WE ARE ALL PERFECTLY FINE

We Are All Perfectly Fine

A Memoir of Love, Medicine and Healing

JILLIAN HORTON, M.D.

HarperCollinsPublishersLtd

HarperCollins books may be purchased for educational, business or sales promotional use through our Special Markets Department.

HarperCollins Publishers Ltd
Bay Adelaide Centre, East Tower
22 Adelaide Street West, 41st Floor
Toronto, Ontario, Canada
M5H 4E3

www.harpercollins.ca

Library and Archives Canada Cataloguing in Publication

Title: We are all perfectly fine : a memoir of love, medicine and healing / Jillian Horton, M.D.
Names: Horton, Jillian, 1974- author.
Identifiers: Canadiana (print) 20200386689 | Canadiana (ebook) 20200386840
ISBN 9781443461634 (hardcover) | ISBN 9781443461641 (softcover) | ISBN 9781443461658 (ebook)
Subjects: LCSH: Horton, Jillian, 1974- | LCSH: Physicians—Canada—Biography. | LCSH: Physicians—Psychology. | LCSH: Burn out (Psychology) | LCSH: Job stress. | LCGFT: Autobiographies.
Classification: LCC R464.H67 A3 2021 | DDC 610.92—dc23

Printed and bound in the United States of America
LSC/H 9 8 7 6 5 4

For Wendy

My baby has not lived in vain. His life has been what it is to all of us, education and development.
—Samuel Taylor Coleridge, on the death of his son Berkeley, in a letter to Thomas Poole, April 6, 1799

ONE

The Curse of Knowledge

I know how I'm going to die.

It's in a tin can of a plane at an altitude so low that birds will see the whites of my eyes as I go down screaming. Whichever nondescript great lake abuts Toronto and Rochester—okay, Lake Ontario—that's the lake I'm dying in, today, on this plane.

The whine of the motor is deafening. The low-pitch pulsing sounds like the apocalypse. Just after takeoff, I snapped a photo of an ominous dent on one of the wings, and I'm wondering whether it will upload to the Cloud if I'm in airplane mode when we crash. Then the Transportation Security Administration investigators will praise me: *One passenger, in a final heroic act, had the presence of mind to leave behind the photographic evidence that unlocked this case for us.*

But that was stupid. A better final act would have been to alert the pilot before takeoff, and then maybe it wouldn't have *been* a final act. And my *final* final act should have been to text my husband to tell him and the kids how much I love them. Or at least go into efficient doctor mode to remind him the youngest is due for a dentist appointment, and please follow up with the roofing company to patch the outrageously massive hole a squirrel chewed in the side of our chimney. Lest we get more squirrels.

By the way, I love you.

I'm a general internist, the kind of doctor who looks after people with medical problems that sound made up. Typhlitis. Neurocysticercosis. Ankylosing spondylitis. I also treat people with less exotic problems but lots of them at once. Heart failure and liver disease and sick kidneys. Stroke and pneumonia and severe mental illness. I work in an inner-city hospital, a rambling facility in need of a paint job, built on Indigenous land in a part of Canada that Truth and Reconciliation seems to have forgotten, a hundred miles from the town where I grew up. I look after people who are sick enough to be in the hospital. Some are dying. Many are homeless. Many are Indigenous and have been subjected to gross, almost unfathomable injustice, racial oppression and intergenerational trauma. They struggle to escape its legacy, which often comes in the form of drug and alcohol addiction.

I'm heading to a place in New York called Chapin Mill. Nobody's sending me. I'm going of my own volition, unsure as to why, doubtful it will make any difference. In the only-in-my-mind major motion picture version of my life, either Hawkeye Pierce or the soulful doctor played by George Clooney on *ER* have staged an intervention, since it's so painfully obvious to viewers that I'm floundering emotionally and need to go away somewhere for at least part of one season.

Interventions don't happen in medicine, in my experience. When they do, they're a late-stage measure, akin to chemotherapy for advanced-cancer patients who have no hope of cure. Most doctors look fine, perennially, until the day they don't. That's because doctors are excellent at compartmentalizing. We are also compliant and conscientious and rigidly perfectionistic, characteristics that put us at risk for choking to death on our own misery—or more specifically, overdosing on the perfect fatal combination of pills, throwing ourselves off just-tall-enough buildings, or slitting open the large arteries we studied so carefully when we were undergraduates, with the sleight of hand to bleed out quickly—if all goes well, in approximately five minutes.

I talk about death a lot; wouldn't you? I'm surrounded by it. I've signed more death certificates than cheques, and I pay for *everything* by cheque. Doctors have a delusional relationship with death. We trick ourselves into the professional assumption that death is reasonable. Not benevolent, but not unpredictable—nothing psycho about it. Birth on a good day is a Hitchcock film; death is often quiet, understated, like dealing with your accountant. So when it shows up on our doorstep, whether for us or one of our family members, suddenly this "reasonable" death that seemed so calm and inevitable when it was happening to other people turns out to be a real handful, and we're often woefully unprepared to deal with it.

But we also talk and think so much about death because medicine is so fucking hard.

I know many jobs are hard. Try being a soldier deployed in Afghanistan. Try being a police officer on the frontlines of the meth crisis. My friend Al is a pharmacist. Believe me, pharmacists have their problems too. All that working with doctors, some of them

5

notorious jerks. All that worrying—are you missing interactions between the red pill and the yellow, or the blue and the white? All those drugs, spread out in front of you like Dylan's Candy Bar minus the carbs. One pill might take the edge off. Just the edge. What if it found its way into your pocket? What if you slipped it under your tongue? Just one. What's the harm? That's why they call it *the edge*, of course. Nothing begins *in medias res*. Every addiction, every dysfunctional behaviour—all of it starts somewhere.

Al and his wife came with us to the beach this past summer. We watched the kids wade out a mile into the shallowest part of Lake Winnipeg, far enough that they were dots halfway to the horizon but the water was still only up to their knees. It was so hot that it made Al think of his first summer job. He worked at a grill, cooking meat. Behind the grill was hotter than any beach. Sometimes Al got assigned to onions. He would stand next to the sink, slicing them, working his way through an entire mesh bag. For the first ten minutes, tears would pour down his face, and his eyes would burn. Every minute was worse than the one before. Just when he thought he couldn't stand it anymore, even though he hadn't finished cutting, the burning stopped. His face was wet with tears, but he couldn't feel anything. He didn't even know he'd been crying.

Al cutting those onions is like me and medicine. In the first few years, everything burned. Then one day the pain just stopped. That was a warning sign, and I missed it. Pain serves a purpose in our lives, sending messages to keep us out of danger. When we ignore those messages, or when our nerves have been damaged by prolonged toxic exposure and we no longer feel any pain, we mistake our insensibility for infallibility. And that's when we can end up in serious trouble.

I didn't know what I was in for when I decided to go to medical school. I knew there was risk; I didn't know the degree. Nobody would climb Mount Everest if they knew unequivocally that once they were at the top, their skin would freeze, and they'd be left with a hideous chunk of black flesh where their face used to be.

And yet, I love being a doctor. There is something so intimate, so fateful between me and medicine. Itzhak Perlman picks up the violin and knows it belongs in his hand. When I sit down at a bedside with a person in pain, there's a moment of deep resonance and grace: everything in my life has led me to that chair. But relationships have undertones, just like instruments. Perlman plays a concert, and it's easy to forget he spent his life making what he does look effortless. And we have no idea what happened in rehearsals.

Why did I go to medical school? I went because of my sister, Wendy. She was the first of four siblings, twelve years older than the youngest (me), an age gap that would normally mean I might have been babysitting her kids before I was out of high school. But six years before I was born, Wendy was diagnosed with brain cancer. Surgeons cut her head open and took the tumour out. If it had been diagnosed earlier, or if that had been the end of it, she might have recovered and had a good life. Instead, just a few days after surgery, her skull still wrapped in Frankenstein bandages, she got post-operative meningitis, an infection of the thin, glistening tissues that encase the brain like a tough layer of Saran wrap. That infection caused swelling, and scarring, and left her with the most complex cluster of disabilities imaginable. It made her the world's most cantankerous disabled person, but also one of its funniest. She was a martini of a human you could never mix again. But her disabilities were so profound that all the doctors advised my parents to stick her in an institution that by today's standards wouldn't even pass for an animal shelter. My mom remembers a doctor, famous in these parts when he was alive, drawing a pie graph on a chalkboard, with a single narrow line representing the one child out of a hundred who survived pediatric anaplastic astrocytoma, then thrusting Wendy's scans up on a lightbox and screaming at my mom and dad, who had asked about her prognosis, "Can't you people get it through your heads? The problem is *there's no brain left*."

But the problem had nothing to do with my parents, or their heads. Doctors were the ones who screwed up my sister's case at the beginning, middle and end. First, there was an unfathomable two-year delay until her diagnosis. Trip after trip to the clinic, my mother's panic rising, because she knew, as mothers often do, that something wasn't right. Wendy's head in those photos from before the surgery, big as a dandelion gone to seed. Vomiting in the morning, bile arcing across the room, bits of her breakfast stuck to the walls. We learn early in medical school that this is called projectile vomiting. It's a classic sign of raised intracranial pressure, along with headaches, balance problems, and deep, intractable nausea, a syndrome you should be able to describe if not diagnose by the time you're in your third year of medicine. Wendy had all these signs. Doctor after doctor missed them. Then, after the diagnosis and the surgery, other doctors had the audacity to yell at my parents that *they* were the ones with something wrong with their heads, despite the fact that my sister, who had gone into the OR looking like a dandelion but otherwise a perfectly regular six-year-old, came out of that operation with a head full of scrambled eggs. My mom always said she could have written a book—but who could bear to read it?

And yet, my parents came across some good people, a few doctors scattered among them. The kind pediatric neurologist in another city who made the correct diagnosis in a few minutes with a simple, thorough physical exam, hardly able to conceal his horror at what his colleagues had somehow missed. A surgeon at the children's hospital, empathetic and skilled, who probably saved her life. And Wendy's last family doctor, a woman who treated Wendy and my elderly parents with compassion and love, offering care in the tradition of the Greek God Asclepius, healing as art.

The narrow line on the pie graph that doctor had drawn for my parents—it wasn't the average survival of one child out of a hundred. That line was a crack my mother and father found or made, then pried open, then somehow managed to just barely squeeze my sister through. My grandmother once said to me, in a voice that didn't reveal whether she thought it was a good thing, "Wendy lived by your mother's will alone." *Nobody* thought she would live. And when she did live, nobody thought her life was worth anything, that it served any purpose; and it was as if the entire medical system was angry at my parents for exposing its shortcomings, angry at Wendy, first for evading diagnosis and then for having the nerve to live when they declared it impossible with, as that one doctor so eloquently put it, no brain left. Much of her was hidden from view, or clouded by fits of intense, uncontrollable rage. But then our Wendy would emerge, hilarious, original, mesmerizing, and you were reminded she had always been there, and you could forget she had been pulverizing you a few minutes earlier because she was pissed you put mayonnaise in her sandwich, because to her mayonnaise was the most disgusting substance on the planet—although I am pretty sure she never had bubble tea—and any anger you had felt would be replaced by love and forgiveness. And then by grief for everything she had lost through no fault of her own, and, maybe as an afterthought, for everything you had lost too.

Later on, once she was an adult, a lot of "experts" told my parents she should just be in a nursing home. They didn't really consider that she had nothing in common with Second World War veterans, or grandmothers who like to knit afghans, or people with dementia who care for rubber dolls as if they're real babies. And her brain injury, specifically the damage to her frontal lobe, the part of the brain that sanitizes thoughts before they come out of your mouth, meant Wendy was liable to say, in a slow but intelligible voice, "Why is that idiot [your sweet grandmother with dementia] carrying that stupid doll," or, "Why is that moron [your adorable grandfather, the Second World War veteran] smoking that disgusting cigarette?"

Life with her was a trial, infinitely more difficult than medical school. It was difficult because it was uncertain, and because there was no end in sight. That tumour decimated many important parts of her and, worse still, left her with the memory of what it had been like to look and move and eat and talk like everybody else. Most people only saw what was gone. They didn't understand anything about her, or about the reality of living with a person who was profoundly disabled in such unique ways.

I didn't understand that reality either. When I was eight or nine, one day at recess, with the air of a child's confession, I blurted out to a teacher, "My family isn't normal." The teacher paused, then looked up and blew her whistle at a pair of boys who were rolling on top of each other like kittens. Before she went to pull them apart, she looked back at me and sighed. She said: "Show me a normal family in this day and age!"

She probably thought she was helping, but that day I started thinking it must be normal to feel like a gaping hole had been blown in your heart. My sister's propped-up shell in a wheelchair, her constant screaming at night, the blaring TV, the cranked-up radio, the complex toileting, the holes in the wall where Wendy's head had gone through the plaster because she couldn't remember that her balance was too poor to walk, the lack of respite, the lack of appropriate medical care, the lack of a single person of any stripe coming to let my parents lie down or to take me and my other sister and brother out to a movie or to the mall, the little extended family we did have too far away or too busy with their own lives to tend to the chronic emergency of ours.

I have a haunting memory, from when I was five, of my mom at the end of the hall, crying that she couldn't take it anymore, my dad telling me in a firm voice to go away, that everything was fine.

So even when my brother developed a febrile illness and a sudden-onset psychosis at the age of fifteen and went permanently to the psychiatric hospital, even when my older sister, Heather, listened to the same depressing record all night with her bedroom door locked, even if I felt like I lived in a Salvador Dali painting, there wasn't cause for alarm. *Show me a normal family in this day and age!*

Years later I would spend an inordinate amount of time seeing a psychologist, and she would tell me exactly two useful things. She would say: "Your sister was your first patient." And she would say that the worst part about what happened to my family is there was nobody to be angry at, because it was nobody's fault.

But she was wrong. I found somebody to get angry at. I had enemies and decided to hold them close, closer than anyone, so close I became one of them, infiltrated their ranks in order to make them pay for what they had done to our family.

I became a doctor.

o o o

Now, ALL THESE years later, I'm on a plane with a phone full of potential forensic evidence, bracing for the impact that has already happened in my mind. The last year has been hard and dark, thumbnails of the same day sketched over and over with a black crayon. Everything has been an effort. The bitter cold all winter. The interminable drive to the hospital and back. The long, windowless hallways. Colleagues I've worked with for ten years who don't even say hello when we pass in the corridors. Going to the ward, finding the right charts, logging in to yet another new electronic health record platform, trying to remember which massive drop-down menu is hiding the discharge note I want to review. Choosing which patients to see from a list already too long to be safe. Finding forms to fill out, ordering tests, four calls coming in on my pager. Five nurses and two students asking me questions, giving me information I can't process, because I'm still trying to find the drop-down menu that will yield the note summarizing the three-month community hospital admission of a woman with fifteen medical problems. Six emails when I dare to check my phone, three about improving the learning environment.

The *learning* environment! What about the teaching environment? There was a time when I loved teaching so much I couldn't wait to get to work. A time when this line from the Hippocratic Oath was almost as precious to me as my marriage vows. *I will*

gladly share such knowledge as is mine with those who are to follow.
Now I am drowning in this water, and I don't want anyone to follow
me into it. Sometimes I just want the students and Hippocrates
and everybody else to leave me the fuck alone.

o   o   o

ONCE A MONTH, if our schedules align, my friends Frank and
Len and I go for coffee in the hospital atrium. We watch the wind
picking up outside, leaves gathering by the glass. We are all in or
near our forties, parents of little boys, internists of some stripe,
sleep-deprived and struggling with an amorphous discontent that
has become medicine's secret ailment. We're good doctors; we
care about our patients. But there's a force bigger than us pushing us to the brink, and some days I'm afraid one of us is going to
tumble over that edge.

I don't tell my friends what's going on with me at this point
since they're basically in the same boat. I don't burden them with
the fact that I'm not sleeping enough, that a constant weight on
my chest like a barbell is making it tough to get through not only
rounds but also supper and playdates and grocery shopping. The
radio in my head is set to perpetual glum, Nespresso pods strewn
across my desk like drugs and paraphernalia I am relying on to get
me through the week on call. Between seeing clusters of patients, I
curl up like a caterpillar in a stained armchair in the corner of my
office, swallowing against the lump in my throat. There's a tingling
behind my eyes, a feeling I get in my mouth, an ache in the teeth
like winter or an empty parking garage. Still, silent, heavy. Boiling
the kettle for tea, momentarily comforted by the smell of chai, a
whiff of spice, the hint of a kitchen at Thanksgiving. My office has

a thin, high band of windows, and they face a brick wall; the effect is like looking up from a well. I am at the bottom of that well. But doctors look fine until the very end. This is a silent emergency, and even if the people around me can smell something burning, none of us has made the connection that the thing on fire is me.

○ ○ ○

THE MORNING BEFORE I left for Chapin Mill, my husband, Eric, and I dropped our three sons off at school. As we stood at the lockers, a little girl came running down the hallway, wisps of hair stuck in her mouth. Her face shone with important news.

"The egg hatched!" she shouted at us. "There's a baby dove!"

My boys went wide-eyed. They kicked off their boots and ran in their socks towards the classroom. Children were gathered around a birdcage. A male dove sat up top, perched on a little trapeze, sounding guttural, excited notes. Below him, a female was sitting on a minuscule body.

The teacher was peering into the bottom of the cage, craning her neck for a good look at the littlest bird. "I don't know if it's alive," she said softly. But a second after she spoke, the baby dove turned its head to the side, extending its translucent neck, its eyelids fused shut. The mother nipped at its hairless body. The children huddled around the cage, transfixed and silent.

On the way back out to the car, I saw geese lined up in a lazy V overhead, their two-tone honking reminding me of the rubber horn I had on my bike when I was a little girl. I felt a pressure in my chest, like a small hand squeezing my heart. The bird had barely moved. *Of course* it was going to die. The mother didn't have a coach or a public health nurse or a doula, and the father was thinking about how soon he could knock her up with another egg. Soon there would be a latex glove, the teacher moving the mother aside as she pried the little dove's body out from under her.

It's a burden, knowing what's going to happen when everyone else is still ten steps back, saying "ooh" and "aah" and calling it a miracle.

That's the curse of knowledge.

o o o

So HOW DID I end up on this plane? A friend who is a social worker invited me to a talk by another friend of hers, a doctor she had invited to speak about mindfulness. I went because my friend phoned me twice, and I wanted to show her I was open-minded, even if I wasn't. I sat in the back row with my jacket over my shoulders. I said it was because I was cold, but really I was waiting for a chance to slip out of the room.

Except it was actually kind of an interesting talk. The speaker's name was Mick Krasner. He was bald and looked more like a beat poet than a doctor. He and his colleagues had published a study in the *Journal of the American Medical Association* showing that their mindfulness program made doctors feel happier and more able to handle the stress of medicine. I had expected him to be a hippie or a freak, but Mick seemed like a lighter, happier version of me from a time before the connections between necessary pieces of myself got severed.

When the talk was over, my friend walked me up to Mick.

"This is the colleague I told you about," she said to him.

Mick smiled. He gave me his card. He suggested I might like to come spend a few days with him and one of his colleagues at a retreat for doctors. There was one in April. He said they still had room at Chapin Mill. He hoped I could join them.

"Is it, like, a *padded* room?"

Mick laughed. "No, but it's a Zen retreat. Lots of cushions."

"I don't think it would help me."

He winked. "Only one way to find out."

Normally this exchange would have irritated me, but that day Mick's words hung in the air, stayed with me on my way home, and lingered that night as I was getting ready for bed.

I lay in the dark, and I knew: this was my Hawkeye/Clooney moment. Mick and my friend were throwing me the only intervention I was ever going to get.

A week later I told my husband I was going to spend five days with a doctor who looked like a beat poet, and I booked a ticket to Rochester.

I made the connection: the thing on fire is me. That's why I'm going to Chapin Mill.

2

The Glass Cliff

The shuttle from Rochester airport is much smoother than death's personal airplane. It travels over tidy roads through sleepy-looking smatterings of houses. Swings, empty of children. A geriatric-looking dog, too tired to bark when the shuttle slows down and turns onto a rural gravel road, descending into forest. I see a pond. A bridge with a mill comes into view, then a littler footbridge over a thin, sparkling stream, like the one where Siddhartha found the meaning of his life. The van stops in front of a wooden building that looks like a cross between a summer camp, Thoreau's cabin and a rustic sanitorium.

I hoist my suitcase down to the ground. It's heavy. There's never a trip when I don't bring more than I need. I've been up since 4 a.m. A halo of light surrounds everything I look at directly. I'm getting a migraine. I wheel my bag through the open glass doors.

A woman greets me at a small table. She asks my name, finds me in a sea of plastic nametags.

17

"How was your trip?"

"Hellish."

She smiles. "Well, that's behind you now. Your room is to the left, down the stairs and on the right."

That's behind you now.

There's an eerie calm in this lobby. People are speaking in hushed voices. I'm stuck here for five days with what I'm going to guess is seriously crap Wi-Fi. I fear this might be a place for absolute weirdos.

My fear has nothing to do with meditation or Buddhists, by the way. They're no weirder than anyone else. But how do you mix Buddhism with the reality of practising medicine? It's like setting Hello Kitty up on a blind date with Darth Vader. That will not end well.

I go to the right, down the stairs, make a left and end up in what looks like Santa's workshop. Damn, I had no idea American Buddhists were so into crafts. I go back up the stairs and make the left I was supposed to make the first time. I find my room. My name is on the door, on a little index card.

There's next to nothing in here. A bed, a chair, a nightstand with a lamp. A wool blanket. A window with slat blinds that have diced the afternoon light into matchsticks. I pull the cord, and the slats rise, revealing a grass-covered hill. Behind it is dark, dense forest. I set my things down on the floor, open the binder the woman handed me at the desk.

Welcome to Chapin Mill.

No flesh foods.

Absolutely no alcohol.

Lights out at 10 p.m.

It dawns on me—I mean, *really* dawns on me.

This is Doctor Rehab.

I sit down on the edge of the bed, perplexed. Then I'm perplexed that I'm perplexed. What did I *think* I'd be doing here? I keep looking out at that little hill, like the top of a viridian baby head. How did I get here? Via a plane unfit for any human. Literally and metaphorically.

But I know exactly what got me here. Twenty years of a toxic culture, twenty years of sleeping with the enemy, of saying "I'm fine" every time I wasn't. Twenty years of shoving the snake back down into the can every time it popped up. Half a lifetime. Half of mine, anyway.

o o o

MEDICINE BEING AS difficult as I've said it is, nobody should be surprised that med schools need people who function like psychiatrists for students who need to be kept from running in the wrong direction or basically combusting in real time. At my school, for the last four years, that person, the associate dean of student affairs, was me.

Deans and university presidents are overwhelmingly men, but the position of associate dean of student affairs is one more frequently bestowed on women. I don't know if this is because women are supposed to be more nurturing, or if it's just assumed that we'll put up with more. My colleague Joanne called it a "glass cliff" job.

But in some ways, when I started it was my dream job. I wanted to develop the character of students, to help build a culture of compassion and kindness, because I believed if I did, none of them would end up screaming at the mother of a little girl with a brain tumour that the girl had no brain left. I wanted to help students understand that if becoming a doctor is like climbing Mount Everest, medical school is only base camp. Their best shot at getting down from the summit alive involves learning to dress for the weather and finding out how to deal with the psychological pressures that rise as the temperature drops. Nobody taught me any of those things. I learned them myself, at the expense of parts of me that ended up frozen and left behind. As a dean, I wanted to be the sort who doesn't make you feel the problem is all about you. I told students I had also struggled on that mountain, also had times when I didn't know if I'd make it down, times when I thought, *My God, what have I done?*

I loved my students without reserve. I loved the hours when I got to lecture them about what being a doctor means to me. I loved supervising them on the wards, taking them from bedside to bedside, encouraging them to hold hands, listen with kindness, talk to patients like they would to cherished friends. I loved showing them how to broach tender subjects in difficult moments, coaching them to find the right words at the right time. I loved debriefing them after something went wrong or someone died, sitting with them in a corner of the nursing station, watching them choke back tears, telling them it's all right to cry. Being an associate dean gave me a platform to protect students who were often vulnerable to systemic abuse in medical education, to offer them protection, producing a compassionate and emotionally intelligent result. I thought I'd found my life's work.

What does an associate dean of student affairs at a medical school actually do? Provide career counselling. Offer crisis support. Grant deferrals. Meet with struggling or failing students.

Sit on committee after committee, council after council. Meet with people who are suffering from anxiety, or depression, whose parents are ill, whose siblings are ill, whose spouses are ill, who have just had their first patient death, or made their first medical error, or delivered their first stillbirth. Encourage. Soothe. Ground in reality. Cheer and motivate. Advocate. Stand up and speak up for those who've been abused or harassed, go after the abusers. Prevent them from harming themselves. Prevent them from harming anyone else. Say things that they will not particularly want to hear, sometimes things nobody else will have the heart or courage to tell them.

My inbox bore witness to the unrelenting nature of the work. It was a constant flood of emails about anxiety and maxed-out credit cards and mental health crises and pregnancies and emergency relationship problems. I responded to it all, in real time. I sent out search parties for students who didn't show up for exams, waited anxiously by the phone until I knew they were okay. I approved enough mental health days to fill a couple of calendars. I granted exam deferrals triggered by a mysterious number of car breakdowns, including some for people I suspected actually had no car. When they failed exams, they wept in my office. When their tears were dry, I helped them pick themselves up again. All this on top of being a clinician, looking after profoundly ill patients in the hospital, huge numbers of them, for weeks at a time, still taking students' calls and answering their emails in between resuscitating people and telling other people they were HIV positive or were going to need dialysis or their cancer had returned.

Some days, my three kids and my husband were barely more than footnotes.

I also met with students who were not particularly wonderful or grateful. In fact, those individuals tended to request far more appointments than all the others combined. I had plenty of emails from those who clearly hadn't heard of Google. They wanted me to help them sign up for Zumba, or clarinet lessons to enhance their "wellness." There were emails to make me "aware" of a strong chlorine taste in the east wing drinking fountain and of fruit flies in the fridge in the student lounge. This associate dean didn't give a flying fuck about fountains or fruit flies; she did very much care about the kind of people we were trying to turn into doctors.

o o o

THEN, A PALPABLE shift. A few years into the job, I started asking students to provide notes for exam deferrals because the number of requests was reaching double digits each week, wreaking havoc on the admin staff and the budget for proctors. Students didn't like their exam schedules, didn't like their *exams*. Felt that medicine shouldn't infringe on their wellness, at any time or in any way, as if the associate dean's job was not to help make medical education safer and more humane but to make it more convenient for them personally—not so much level the playing field as raze the mountain.

I was hearing about it from others across the country, but I was feeling it personally every time I set foot in a lecture hall: something was beginning to go rancid. I had always loved telling students the story of my vulnerable sister, how badly she had been failed by the medical system. Now, when students came to my lectures, they sat in the farthest seats at the back, blank faces bathed in white light reflected from laptops, browsers open to Facebook. Maybe it was my imagination, but I thought I heard whispers, saw smirks and snide looks on just enough faces to shut me down inside.

And the wards were no retreat. I'd spend two weeks leading a clinical team, bonding with them, teaching them to listen, to speak with humility, to learn about their patients so they could offer them the treatments that aligned with their values and lives, only to sign over on a Monday to another physician who might well admonish them for wasting so much time talking to patients on rounds when there was "real work" at hand, undoing everything I'd just done.

Education is not inevitably a one-way, top-down hierarchy. Any teacher can be undermined by a couple of colleagues or a big enough student mob, quickly reduced to a punchline. For a woman, there is an even bigger challenge than breaking the glass ceiling, and it is getting caught on the wrong side of a crack in the glass cliff.

My joy had been flickering, and finally it was snuffed out like a match. Suddenly, my work as a teacher felt pointless. My confidence in what I was doing, my certainty about why I was doing it, was obliterated. I lost any desire to make myself vulnerable, to tell the true story about my own climb up the mountain.

I sent the dean an email saying I was quitting. I brought in cardboard boxes and dumped the contents of my drawers into them. Teaching awards. Thank-you cards. "Thank you for always believing in me!" *I didn't always believe in you and I definitely don't right now.* "Thank you for always being there for me!" *Too bad my husband and kids can't say the same.*

It didn't take long to fill those boxes: a terminally ill houseplant, stale Fairmont tea, pictures of my children feeding pigeons in Vancouver, thirty or forty books: Joseph Campbell's *The Hero's*

Journey and *William Osler: A Life in Medicine, The Picture of Dorian Grey* and *Gray's Anatomy*.

On the way out, I passed students in the hallway, some gathered in groups, some not noticing me at all, others looking at me quizzically.

"Hey, you moving, Dr. H.?"

"Spring cleaning, Sam."

"Dr. H., can I help you with anything?"

"Too late for that, Ali, but thanks."

Was I ever that young? Had I ever written letters to my associate dean calling the number of parking spots designated for my program "unacceptable," or the failure to fund sandwiches at interest-group nights a "critical situation in need of rectification, immediately"? No. I couldn't afford a car, and I made my own sandwiches. I was far from perfect, but I never equated having to write two exams in a twelve-hour period, or being asked to name the bones of the hand, with a sentence in a forced labour camp.

And yet, some of the students were good kids. *Such* good kids. How many of them had sat across from me in those chairs in my office, so eerily like me, sending me messages in a bottle from ancient, earlier versions of my own life? Suddenly gifting me with the ability to see something about myself as I was back then—how tough yet fragile, how earnest, how vulnerable, how intent on making a difference. For every kid who treated me like a concierge, there were at least three students who didn't even think they were worth my time, who thought their problems were best handled in silence, on their own, by themselves. Emailing me messages that always started with *I'm so sorry to bother you*, even though they were the people I had intended to be there for in the first place. I had been just like them. I hadn't wanted to bother anyone either. When I was a medical student, it wasn't even clear to me who I would have bothered. If there was a person, other than me, responsible for my overall well-being, I sure didn't know who they were. If anybody had asked, I would always have said I was perfectly fine. It never occurred to me that I had the option to say anything else.

I had just wanted it to be different for these kids.

Everybody Here
Looks Perfectly Normal

All the doctors are gathering in the great room tonight to hear about our schedule for the next five days.

There's a lot of chatter, the din of excited people.

Mick sees me standing by the door and walks over to give me an enormous hug, the hug you give a friend you haven't run into for years. I'm really glad to see him.

"I'm so happy you came." He does sound truly happy.

"Me too, but I'm hoping this isn't a Jonestown kind of thing."

"Too late now."

There are about fifty doctors here. Everyone is milling around, saying polite hellos. Chairs and cushions are spread out in a semicircle. It's obvious that some people are stuck on choosing between chair and cushion, worried about looking stupid. I already look stupid, because I'm at Weirdo Doctor Rehab in the Woods, so I choose a chair.

The doctor who co-leads the program rings a bell. His name is Ron Epstein. I read his book about mindfulness and medicine before getting on the plane. Actually I read half of it, underlined a bunch of things that seemed important in the first few chapters, then started to feel hopeless, which gave way to feeling resentful, because all of it sounded correct, the ideas sounded nice, but it's a bit late for swimming lessons when you're drowning.

The bell's vibrations linger in the room. A theatrical quiet descends.

Who are all these people? Men and women, all ages, all colours. Nametags that say Boston and Texas and Montreal and Australia. All screwed-up doctors, just like me?

Ron welcomes us. He talks about what we'll do over the next five days, how we'll spend our time together. He advises us to leave our phones in our rooms and tell people we can't be reached, but this seems like a step away from Hare Krishna. I'm keeping mine in my pocket.

There will be a lot of sitting. We'll push each other, and we'll support each other. We'll create a community.

Do I *do* community?

For the next ten minutes, Ron says, we should talk about why we're here.

We drag our chairs into small groups, clustering around tables. People speak self-consciously. Some ramble. Some only say a little, fumbling on a handful of words.

I'm totally burnt out.

I don't enjoy things anymore.

Gotta get back to my factory settings.

I'm hoping something can remind me why I became a doctor.

I lost my husband.

28

I'd like to care again.

We move around to other tables. We say the same things to other people, answering the same question again but choosing different words.

I'm not present in my life.

I feel so disappointed.

I want to figure out whether this still matters to me.

I'm looking for something to make me feel better.

I study these people. It's too early for me to tell whether anybody else in the room is more or less screwed up than I am. They mostly look perfectly normal. I suspect I do too, aside from my hair. A bit of bright blue interspersed with the rest of my brown mop is my shark's fin, my signal that I'm just a little unpredictable. A signifier. Or maybe it's a warning.

I think about my boys, wonder what they're doing, picture them in their little pyjamas, with damp hair and storybooks. A rush of longing. Breath, caught in my throat. Eric putting them to bed, brushing their wet curls aside, kissing their cheeks as he settles them in. That visceral need for them to be in my arms, pressed into my body, their faces against the crook of my neck, little chests rising and falling against my sternum. The smell of their heads. The little whorl of hair in the centre of their scalps, curving like markings on a lollipop.

I'm a good-enough mother, but I'd like to be a better one. Not a mother who bakes her own sourdough or holds a Food Channel–calibre birthday party, just one whose mind is in the same place as her body, who isn't thinking about a student or a patient or a lab value while reading *Frog and Toad*.

Why am I here? Why are any of these people here?

If medicine and I were in couples therapy, I'd confess that I still love it. I really do. It's written on my heart in indelible ink, next to the names of my husband and children and the rest of my family. Loving it isn't voluntary; it's reflexive for me, the connective tissue between who I am and what my heart drives me to do in the world.

So why am I here?

I'm here because Mick invited me, Ron.

Why am I here?

I'm here because Siddhartha found everything in his life in a stream. The meaning of his life. The sound of the water like a chorus of children. The sweetness of human voices. Maybe I will too.

Why am I here?

I'm here because medicine has left me a little bit broken. I'm here because I'm not really here anymore, haven't been for a long time.

Because I would like to find a way back into my life.

4

Committed

I don't remember anything about my first day of medical school. The room it was in, who I sat with, what was on my mind. I do remember that, at several points, I was thinking, *shit*. It seemed as if I'd made a big, terrifying mistake. I knew how to dissect a sonnet, not a cadaver. I tell medical students I remember what it was like to be in their shoes, but back then I actually felt as if I wasn't wearing shoes or anything else. I felt naked.

I went to a medical school called McMaster. It was and still is a cutting-edge and world-renowned place, started in the '70s by idealistic, intellectual hippies who were upset at how antiseptic medical education had become. My hazy early memories of Mac have been replaced by a more generic mood memory, a visual Muzak centred around the edgy '70s lecture hall, with its angular lines and palette of greens. There is the odd specific: a formalde-hyde tear leaking out of a cadaver's closed eye in the anatomy lab. A young boy with a neck mass. A woman with seizures and a thick, grey, rope-like braid down to her waist. A windowless call room. A pager that felt like a live grenade. A constant sensation of being in an elevator prone, without warning, to sudden drops.

There were good times, though—moments with friends, spells of laughter and deep connection. Nights in the medical lounges, eating together, debriefing, plotting, commiserating. Hours spent with patients who made me laugh and cry. Sara on Pediatrics, a toddler with Down syndrome who banged her metal cup on the siderails of her bed every morning when I came to see her. Ellie on Psychiatry, who whispered to me that when she was a kid she saw a funnel cloud and tried to ride her bike into it. Fanny on Internal Medicine, an elderly Jewish lady with a leaky heart valve who invited me to her retirement home for bacon sandwiches. She never married, had no children. She took such an interest in me, divining my Ashkenazi roots, stroking my hand, asking about my studies, saying how proud my parents must be of everything I'd done. When she was discharged, she slipped me her address on the back of a hospital menu. I tacked it up onto the bulletin board in my bedroom, planning to write her in a few weeks. When I finally did, I sent her a funny card, saying I hoped she was doing well and that her heart was behaving itself, hoped I hadn't missed the window for a visit. A letter showed up in my mailbox a few weeks later from something called National Trust. I didn't even open it at first, thinking they were a bank wanting to lend me money because I was a medical student. When I finally slit it open, I was surprised to see it was from a lawyer.

We are the executors of the will of Fanny Stein. We are sorry to tell you that Fanny died on November 12th. As such we offer our condolences on the loss of your friend.

I felt a painful lump in my throat. I looked at that word on the paper for a long time: *friend*. This was around the time a new term was beginning to appear in medicine, professionalism—a word that would fundamentally alter the doctor–patient relationship in both intended and unintended ways.

Was Fanny my friend?

Actually, yes. Yes, she was.

That was my first small act of resistance. I folded the letter away for safekeeping.

o o o

FROM THE TIME we started in clinical rotations as medical students, all of us were basically incarcerated for an average of seven years of training. We spent more time in hospitals than out of them. You might argue with the word *incarcerated*, but it would be less wrong than you'd think. Medical students, residents and prisoners wear uniforms, eat bland food, have limited contact with the outside world, and inhabit a hierarchical culture. I got paroled the day my fellowship ended, on June 30, 2004. It was Eric's birthday. I walked out into the sun, squinting, waiting on the curb for him to meet me, so we could take the subway home together and begin our new life.

But I struggled after my training, just as many prisoners struggle to adjust to life after incarceration. Some of them never really adjust and intentionally get themselves sent back to jail, because jail is familiar—awful but contained. Even the worst possible place can engender a feeling of security if it seems easier to navigate than a bigger place with more uncertainty. The outside world has no margins, no structure. We get to know jail so well that we forget what made us want to live in the world outside its walls. Our reference points are permanently altered. We lose the ability to recognize normal.

Over the years, I learned that many of my friends in medicine struggled too. We never exactly got used to life on the outside. It became another channel, a dual track, a world that was always quietly summoning us back to a place where the people around us could understand our words, our humour, our rituals. It was easier to be in that place. It started to seem like the only *real* world. In a patient, we would have recognized that kind of confusion as a symptom of mental illness. In medicine, without a trace of irony, we called it being committed.

o   o   o

JUST AS THINGS were starting to get unpalatable for me as an associate dean, but before they became intolerable and I quit, I was passing through Toronto, where I had done my residency. A colleague asked if I would come give a talk to the internal medicine residents. I said sure. The chief resident, Nikki, met me at the elevator.

She takes me to set up in the rounds room. Residents straggle in. Some of the young men have a fidgety, cocky energy. The girls are mostly impossibly thin, wearing gauzy pants and shirts.

I fiddle with the laptop, set up my PowerPoints. The city is fourteen stories below. Nikki introduces me while the students are descending on plates of sandwiches. I have to compete with tuna salad.

"Thanks, Nikki. It's such a strange feeling to be back here. Exhilarating too. But when I was here, I was suffering. I feel like nobody talks about that."

I tell them a bit about my training. Then I talk about burnout. I show them some comics by doctors, including one I wrote.

"This is another medium for us to tell stories, and it's super-efficient. It's hard to believe, but we actually process images 60,000 times faster than words."

I take stock of the room. Every single person in the room is looking at their phones.

I pause for a minute. "Speaking of images, I'm noticing that you guys are all on your phones."

Startled, they look up in unison.

"I'm live-tweeting this," says a girl. "What's your handle?"

"I don't tweet."

A hand shoots up in the corner. "Don't you feel like you *need* an online presence?"

"I prefer actual presence."

I see a few smiles, people exchanging looks of comprehension.

Nikki puts up her hand. "You do kind of have an online presence, though, right? You write that column, 'Midlife with Dr. Horton'?"

"It's called 'Med Life'!" I correct her quickly. Everybody is laughing. I feel myself blushing. "Don't you guys feel like online presence is crap?"

"How do you build a career, then?"

"You do that in person! At meetings and talking to people!"

The room is uncomfortable. I'm Grandpa Simpson yelling at a cloud, explaining how things used to be in my day. I'm just over forty, for God's sake. How can the gulf between me and these kids be so vast as to be impassable?

"No offence," says a curly-haired resident in the corner. "I think things are different now, and it's hard for older people to understand."

"I'm not old! I'm just over forty!" They all laugh again. Was that a joke? Did I intend for it to be funny? "My point is, presence means being present. An online presence is an oxymoron. It's like virtual love."

He shrugs. "Virtual love *is* a thing."

Somebody quips from the back of the room, "Dave means porn." Everyone laughs again.

"Okay, I'm going to ignore that. But it's superficial, right? It's not real love. And aren't you just counting who tweets and re-tweets what you say, trying to amplify your own voice?"

The live-tweeter explains it to me patiently. "We totally are, Dr. Horton, because then everybody gets to have their say."

"But if everybody's having their say at the same time . . . how do you hear anybody else?"

"Everybody has a *right* to their say."

"But is what everyone has to say equally valid?"

"It's how we do things now."

"Well, I liked the old way."

"But you said you were suffering when you were here."

Dave, the resident with curly hair, puts up his hand again. "Is it possible you're just idealizing now? Because when we read your column, 'Midlife' or whatever, it doesn't sound like you liked the old normal."

I'm silent for a minute. Nobody speaks. Maybe they're wondering if I'm going to do something adorable, like pull out a Walkman.

"You know what?" I tell them after several more seconds have passed. "You're completely right."

They're quiet, watching me. Maybe they think I'm being sarcastic. Nobody is looking at their phones.

"When I was a resident, it's like I said at the start, nobody talked about burnout. Or suicide, or addiction, or any of that stuff. The staff doctors didn't say anything to us about their lives. So we felt like the problem was *us*. Now that *we're* talking about it, we've stripped you of an illusion. You thought the problem was med school, or residency, right?" Several of them nod vigorously. "But now you're seeing it doesn't end there. We took a silent film and added a soundtrack, and it turned out to be a horror show." I let out a long, slow breath. "I don't think I would have gotten through residency if I didn't think it would get better once it was over. And plus, you guys have the added challenge of technology. It's made some things better, but it's made other things a lot worse."

"But *doesn't* it get better?" a young woman asks. "I mean, you have more control over things when you're staff, right?"

"Yes, but . . . by then you have kids, and aging parents, and families and patients complaining about things, and huge problems with gender imbalance and harassment in leadership if you're a woman or a person of colour, and tenure, and research, and maybe health problems yourself, and huge administrative burdens if you take on roles where you want to try to change the culture. It's a lot. I mean, residency was harder in some ways, but afterwards is . . . really hard too."

I look around at the group. Sandwiches are pushed aside. A few have turned back to their phones, but most are waiting for me to say something reassuring, words that will make it all okay.

"I hope it'll get better," I tell them. "But the truth is that finishing residency is just changing coal mines."

"Well," says Dave, after a long pause, "thanks for being so candid with us."

Nikki stands up. She thanks me on behalf of the group. The students go back to the wards. I apologize to Nikki, feeling sheepish for sounding so negative. Nikki says no, it was really important, and she's grateful for my time, although it's just as plausible she thinks this was a disaster and is thrilled to get rid of me. She steers me towards the elevator the way you dutifully take your grandma to the washroom at a restaurant, shouting in her ear, "It's right here, Grandma. The bathroom is right here." She even pushes the button for me, in case I've forgotten if the street exit is at Ground or Lobby.

When I've reached the right floor and stepped out of the elevator, I pause for a minute in the atrium, watching the long stream of patients trying to find their way, some frail, some apparently well, their bodies hiding secret pathologies, like ticking time bombs. I'm putting my coat on when my phone vibrates with a new email notification. I fish it out of my pocket, read the screen:

> Dr. Horton, thanks for your talk just now. Normally I'd have found you on Twitter ☺, but I got your email from Nikki. I really appreciate your honesty. I just wanted to let you know that I've been struggling with depression, and your talk right now gave me hope.

Holy shit. How did *I* give this person hope? That was the most depressing talk I've ever given.

I guess it's like when you make an elusive diagnosis in a patient who hasn't been feeling well for months. Even if the disease is untreatable, sometimes it's just a relief to hear the truth.

I walk to the lakeshore, a place I used to go on weekends, sometimes with my friend Todd but usually by myself. I settle on a bench among rows of seating near the ferry to Toronto Island. I used to watch the mangy, over-fed gulls and the whitecaps on the water, ferries gliding ghostlike in and out of the terminal, the streetcars in the distance emerging and disappearing into tunnels beneath the ground, everything always in motion, while I sat absolutely still, clinging to the certainty that at least after residency, things were going to get better.

Now, here I am again, looking out at the cold, grey water. The kids were right. This *is* Midlife with Dr. Horton.

And it's beginning to look like a crisis.

Attachment

When you're a doctor, it's tough not to take a history everywhere you go. It's a default mode. You're on an airplane, and there's a person next to you. Soon you're instinctively grilling them. Where are you going? What's in Houston? How long have you lived there? What do you do? Questions tumble out, and before you know it, you've got enough for a clinic note.

At supper, we ask each other questions. We're taking histories, trying to figure out soft hierarchies and groupings. I gravitate towards other internists. We immediately start talking about our practices. Do you do acute care? Inpatient? Where did you train? We're searching for things we have in common, but also looking to assert ourselves relative to who else is here. We find some common threads, limp connections to people we went to school with. Names of old classmates come up, names I haven't heard in twenty years.

Why didn't I keep in touch with more of those people? I may not show it, but there's a raw, unfinished edge inside me, like a knife homemade for a street fight. I use it to cut most cords. I've never gone to a class reunion. I say it's because I don't like good-byes, but the truth is I also don't like hellos because they *lead* to goodbyes. I'll let patients get close, but they usually sort out the logistics for me by disappearing after discharge, or dying. But with most of my friends, I tend to fade over and out, to evade, to never be available for a call, to pass through town without meeting for supper, preferring to be cocooned in a hotel in silence. It's not indifference; it's the opposite of indifference. It's an abundance of emotion, too much resonance, the strain of the memory of love. I'll do anything to avoid that sting, the sharp bite of grief, the anxiety that this might be the last time I'll ever see them. A risk I'm constantly managing.

Where did that come from? When I first left for university, my parents drove me there, leaving Wendy in the care of a tenuous patchwork of respite workers, setting off on the thousand-mile trek through the Canadian Shield via Michigan and along the unforgiving shores of Lake Superior. Getting there, settling in, buying sheets and a fruit bowl and pillows and a silver kettle, things I'd need in my new life. A wave of dread rising, rising, until it was time to say goodbye to my parents. My mother, wearing dark glasses, only the second time in my life I could ever remember seeing her cry, the three of us forming a little circle in the hallway, me regretting everything about this plan, wishing I'd never won a scholarship to this stodgy, faraway place. Then watching from my dormitory window as their Oldsmobile pulled away from the curb, sobbing into my hands and thinking, *What kind of person does this? What kind of person leaves her parents under these circum-*

stances? My sister Heather knew that feeling; she tried to go away once too. She came back after only a year.

Or the summer Wendy moved out of the house for the first time, to a rural hospital that promised to build a small brain injury unit for other young people. Wendy was having none of it. *This is my home! I grew up in this house, and this is where I intend to die.* That's what she said. When moving day finally came, we loaded everything into the van, her clothes, her doll collection, her little china cups. Her jewellery. Her pictures. Her records, her radio, her television. She couldn't grasp any of it, saw it as an utter betrayal. Wendy, incredulous, trying to grab onto my dad's leg as he disconnected the wires to her stereo. *Why do things have to change?* she screamed, the look on her face permanently seared in my memory. *Why can't things just stay the same?*

No wonder goodbyes were a land mine for me. They initiated a cascade of complex emotion that left me drowning. Better to slip out in the night, disappear from people's lives altogether.

o o o

THE WOMAN ACROSS from me is wearing her nametag. *Jodie.* She strikes me as a hybrid of other people I've known and loved: short, sinewy, curls like corkscrews. Soft-spoken but intense, a person whose attention puts you on notice: prepare to get real.

I lean towards her.

"I'm Jill."

"Jodie."

"You remind me of some people I know."

"My condolences to them."

"That's exactly what one of them would say."

43

"Well, why don't you tell me what they'd say next, and you can manage the whole conversation by yourself?"

"Love how introverted you are."

"Good pickup." She takes a bite of some kind of fleshless rice dish. She doesn't look up.

"Why are you here?"

"I'm looking for peace."

"Like, world peace?"

She chews silently for a minute. "Yeah, world peace, idiot."

We grin at each other.

"What's with the blue hair?"

"It's an act of protest."

"Against what?"

"Conformity in medicine."

"Look at you. A rebel with claws."

"What are you? Besides totally disinhibited?"

"GP. You?"

"Internist."

"Outpatient?"

"Inpatient."

"What's that like?"

"Busy. We never turn anybody away, though."

"Neither do we, as long as they have insurance."

"What's *that* like?"

"It's like bullshit." She pushes her plate away. "It's like violence to my soul."

"Have you ever done anything like this before?" She looks at me blankly. "Like, this place."

"Bunch of times. You know about Omega?" I shake my head. "Omega's a good one. Retreat centre. You can go for days."

"Did it help?"

"Help what?"

"Anything."

"Oh, it definitely helped. But you have to want it."

"Well, obviously if you go somewhere like that you want to be helped."

She smiles. "Is that obvious?"

A sudden, urgent thought crosses my mind. "There's coffee here, right?"

"Nope." She watches my face transform into a mask of panic. "Relax, Bluebell. It's by the side door."

"Not funny to joke about coffee."

"Nothing's off-limits here—don't you know that yet?" She squints at my nametag. "Horton?"

I'm starting to figure that out.

6

Sherry with Tutors

Everyone has drifted from the dining hall into their rooms for the night. The complex is quiet. Doors occasionally open, feet pad on the carpet down to washrooms and showers. The lamp on the table casts a small, tidy disc of light. Rain hits the window in staccato bursts. I sit on the bed and lean against the wall, pulling the rough wool blanket over my legs. I'm exhausted, but not ready to sleep. I take a pad of paper and a pen out of my backpack and write, *Why am I here?* But then I cross it out, and instead I write, *Why I am here*, because it sounds more confident and less whiny.

1. *Because I'm not the best mother I can be. When I'm with my boys I'm always thinking about medicine, students, etc. Not present.*
2. *Because I've lost what's best about me and I have to get it back.*

3. *Grief I've never processed.*
4. *Something frozen/broken/blocked.*
5. *Meet other screwed-up doctors who look normal.*
6. *Stuck in state of hatred of entitled students.*
7. *Sleep in room with weird wool blanket.*
8. *Have online shopping delivered to American address to avoid paying duty.*
9. *Start writing again.*

Start writing again. I lay my pen down on the paper. Those words sting.

Plenty of people think they'll be writers. I know that. I loved science, and I was serious about playing piano, but it was literature I chose to study as an undergraduate and then master's student; Plath and Larkin and Ishiguro constantly whispered in my ear for me to come join them. I wanted to live and breathe their craft. I thought about my life in terms of books I'd write, words as a way to change the world. I ended up in a competitive writing studio in the Department of English, surrounded by people who were really, truly serious about writing. The professor, Stan, was an editor at one of the major publishing houses. One day I went to see him during his office hours. I worked up the courage to ask him if he thought I had enough talent to be a professional writer.

"Yep," he said.

I clung to that "yep" for the next twenty-five years.

But Wendy needed me. My parents needed me. And I knew there was something about me that patients needed too. I'd spent two summers working in nursing homes. Playing old songs on an old piano, belting out "The White Cliffs of Dover" for a bunch of people in their nineties and noticing the difference in the room, before and after. And later, drinking tea with them, my hands holding one of theirs, my face up close to their papery ears, that tender intimacy, the same way I leaned in to talk slowly to Wendy so she could hear me. People told me things, confided in me, poured their hearts out. Heather and I had watched *M*A*S*H* obsessively as kids. Secretly, I thought of myself as a carbon copy of Hawkeye Pierce. Just like Hawkeye, even when I didn't know how to ease my own pain, I knew instinctively how to do it for others.

I thought I could still be a writer if I went into medicine. My journals and study notes all have quotes and plots scribbled in the margins. Funny lines, tragic lines, images, moments I never wanted to forget. For the first few months of residency, every day when I wasn't on call, I got up at 5 a.m. so I could write for thirty minutes before work. But soon, those thirty minutes represented a disturbingly large portion of my sleep budget, and scraps of unfinished stories began piling up on the side of my desk until it looked like a paper junkyard. Things got so hard so fast that I just had to focus on living and getting through each day. And before long I was lucky if I could write a postcard. There wasn't a way to be everything to everyone in those years, and the easiest dreams to abandon were my own.

The irony is I might have made the final decision to choose medicine because of a girl I barely knew. She was the type of friend who draws you close so she can cradle you while she tries to slit your throat. We were students in the same faculty of Graduate Studies. One day she asked me what I was going to do after grad school, and I said I was thinking about applying to medicine. McMaster was only a couple hours away, and at the time they had a reputation for taking people like me, people with colourful backgrounds relative to the usual pre-med, degrees beyond the sciences. Their philosophy was that people like me brought a different perspective to medicine—that academic gene pools need students who look at problems in totally different ways. My experiences with Wendy had also given me a particular way of relating to patients and families, a reason for wanting to be a doctor that I thought could make me a strong applicant. But the truth is, I might have just carried on in English if that girl in Graduate Studies hadn't said to me, in her sweet-as-a-poisoned-drink voice, "Maybe you should be careful who you tell you're applying to *medicine*."

Why? Would people think I was selling out?

There was a beat of silence, a smug, expectant look spreading across her face. I realized: This witch doesn't think I can get into medical school.

I could get into med school.

Couldn't I?

I could. I would. I did. But there was a complicating factor. Right after a thick acceptance letter arrived from Mac, another envelope came. This one had a postmark from the U.K. I was being offered a full scholarship to go to Oxford for a PhD in English.

The medical school acceptance letter was printed by a computer; the package from Oxford included a personal invitation on crinkly yellow paper to drink sherry with tutors. I could picture my new Oxford life: I'd have a bike with a basket, and spend hours at the Bodleian. The real white cliffs of Dover. Weekends in Paris. Wool sweaters from the highlands, and a hearth and a stone fireplace older than anyone I had ever met. Bookshelves full of Yeats and Tennyson, and a room of my own, like Virginia Woolf's. A place where the words could pour out of my heart and onto the page, and maybe someday those pages would find their way onto other shelves, maybe even the Bodleian itself.

But lying awake on those tortured, miserable nights, working it all out as if it were a formula with an elusive right answer, the "Go" or "Stay" columns were really "tutors with sherry" versus my sister in her wheelchair, bent over at a forty-five-degree angle, holding her head in her hands and asking if I could please take her to the summer fair. Those tutors wanted to know my interests within postmodernism. My sister had a more basic question for me: *When are you coming home?*

Home. My mom and dad at yet another gate in the airport, watching, waving this time as I boarded the plane that would carry me across an ocean for a year and then another and another. Maybe to marry an Englishman. Maybe never to return.

I didn't need to study English at Oxford to learn the power of words. I'd already had my most important teacher. It was that doctor, yelling at my parents, *There's no brain left.* He taught me that people with power have a duty to speak with care, because they have been entrusted with something fragile they have no right to break. He helped me understand that medicine itself was a very specific kind of power, one I would never, ever abuse, because I knew it was sacred. And anyway, I wasn't drawn to power. I was drawn to medicine because it was my calling, the way a bird is drawn to the song of its own kind.

That was the only contest Wendy won in her whole life. She drew me home. Not out of pity, but out of love and its attendant duty, and a sense there might be things in life that would matter more to me in twenty years than whether I had a PhD from Oxford or had seen the Bodleian. So one day that summer, I was able to look Wendy in the eye and tell her something she would forget a few minutes later: because of her, I was going to be a doctor. And in a few years, I'd be coming home.

TWO

The Step You Don't Want to Take

Next morning I consult the schedule, which says we are starting in the Zendo at 6:30.

Have I read this right? 6:30?

It's 6:10, and I'm only awake because I got up to go to the bathroom. But now I'm aware that around me, doors are opening and
closing. The Zen beehive is coming to life with little doctor work-
er-bees all doing as they're told.

The washroom consists of a white sink and a toilet. Just a canvas of white wall, primed. In the corner, I find a tiny mirror on a
stand, about as useful for looking at your reflection as a Tiffany
locket. I comb my fingers through my hair. My head looks like a
blue toilet brush. But there's no time to wash it unless I want to
be late for the Zendo. Despite not even knowing what a Zendo is.

I go back into my room and look at the map. Zendo is at the back
of the centre. Okay, I can find that. I pull on a tunic and some leg-
gings and join the stream of people padding slowly up the stairs.

Zendo appears to be a place where you don't actually do anything. It's not a great hall so much as a spacious room, with four long rows of seating platforms separated by wide aisles. It's dimly lit. A thin strip of windows runs along the top of all the walls, reminiscent of the tiny ones in my office at the hospital. Outside it's still pitch black. Square, oversized meditation cushions are piled on the seats. There are already people in meditation poses, sitting along the walls, legs crossed, eyes closed. Mick and Ron are up front. There's a metal bowl between them. I want a metal bowl like that filled with coffee.

I find an empty cushion and ease myself up onto the raised platform. The space between the platforms is big enough for a streetcar. Nobody is speaking. I can't share any of my stupid jokes. I always have to be saying something clever.

Something I *think* is clever.

I lower myself onto the cushion, folding in my legs. Jodie is across from me. She's wrapped in a very cool wool shawl and seems to have her hands tucked inside some type of hidden pockets, like it's a meditation straitjacket. Her eyes are closed. She looks like an ad for enlightenment. Meanwhile I still look like a blue toilet brush.

Where am I supposed to put my hands? I let them rest on my quads. Was there an email I missed about bringing your own straitjacket? This actually kind of hurts my back.

"Beginning with the breath." Mick. His words are a surprise in the silence.

"Noticing the breath." Does he have a lisp?

Why am I always with the jokes, even when there's nobody else in here with me?

Is there somebody in here with me?

Mother, is that you?

"The mind will wander. This is what a mind does. When you notice your mind wandering, gently bringing it back, focusing your attention on the breath."

My mind *only* wanders. Something happened to it. I used to be able to learn a Mozart sonata by memory in a week. I had this focus like a laser. Now my mind is more like a Roomba.

"When you're ready, coming into a standing position."

Okay, I like standing, I've got standing. Jodie looks blissed out. She opens her eyes. She nearly caught me looking at her.

Mick says we're going to start walking through the Zendo, forming a line. Hello, comrades! He tells us to go behind the person on our right. I've noticed this guy before; he was at one of my tables last night. He said he was here because he was burnt out. I think his name is Greg. He's older than me, with a little grey goatee like Sigmund Freud, and a North Face sweatshirt.

We start following each other through the Zendo, in a line that moves slowly, then quickly, depending on Mick's instructions. He has us walk purposefully, shifting our weight from left to right, then hurriedly, staying close to the person in front of us. It's funny, noticing the weight shifting from foot to foot, all those small bones able to support the rest of me. How is that even possible? Why didn't I ask that question in medical school? Why has no student ever asked me that, and yet I get ten emails a month demanding to know why the university no longer pays for sandwiches at interest-group nights?

Greg stops abruptly. I slam into him. He almost slams into the person in front of him, and a line of doctor dominoes almost goes down. "Sorry," I say, but he doesn't answer because we're in silence.

Mick tells us to start walking again. This time I'm more careful.

I do notice my breathing. I wonder whether the person behind me is staring at my ass. I hope not. To hell with them if they are. I hear my grandmother's voice, warning me every time she saw me enjoying a cookie when I was a kid that if I ate too much, I'd get an ass like my auntie's. I wasn't even old enough to understand what she meant. Was it a comes-in-the-mail kind of thing, or more like that time she woke up with shingles?

Bring the mind back.

Make the mind great again.

Mick tells us to stop in front of our cushions. I try not to look at Jodie again lest she think I'm a weirdo. We're sitting back down, and I tuck my legs in, balancing on the half-moon pillow in the middle of the big cushion.

We sit for a few minutes longer. Then Mick surprises me by reading a poem.

Start close in,
don't take the second step
or the third,
start with the first
thing
close in,
the step
you don't want to take.

Did Mick write that himself?* It's pretty good. He reads it twice, in case anyone was too dumb to catch it the first time.

---

* I later learned that the poem was by David Whyte: "Start Close In," in *David Whyte: Essentials* and *River Flow: New and Selected Poems* (Washington: Many Rivers Press, 2020 and 2012).

Do I have a first step I don't want to take?

I can't answer that question. I notice how the long, thin windows above Mick and Ron are filling with light, changing colour, yellow, then pink, like urine test strips.

That's gross, Horton.

What would it be, this step I don't want to take?

Finding a way back into my life? I don't even know what that means. Or if that's possible.

Is it possible?

I sort through the thoughts as they come to me in the silence. Some are only half formed.

Something about Wendy, shadowy. Something about medicine, a kind of black-hole feeling tugging me along with it. Writing. Something about writing. All that old cesspool with food.

Forgiveness. Something about forgiveness. *That's the spot.* Like finding the tender point on the abdomen, when a patient suddenly winces, pulls back, everything tightening involuntarily. That spot is where the money is. I'm doing that, inside, as I land on that word.

Who do I need to forgive?

It can't just be the students. They're only the last mile on a long journey.

Mick, I'm going to fail this test. But I know you're onto something, because I'm super uncomfortable, and it isn't just because my quads are getting necrotic from sitting like a pretzel for thirty minutes.

That's when Ron rings the bell, which means we're done, for now. The metallic note lingers in the air. Like one more unanswerable question.

8

The Nausea

Let me get something out of the way.

It's Toronto, and the year is 2000. It's one of the hottest summers on record. Garbage is piled everywhere on curbs, and the city stinks like an inhospitable planet. I've just moved here from a medical school run by brilliant, optimistic hippies, and now I'm at an institution whose culture, rumour has it, eats hippies for breakfast.

I matched to a program in internal medicine. I chose internal because I liked its complexity. I had come within a hair of choosing pediatric neurology, but fortunately at the last minute I seemed to recognize there was a pathology in that choice, a way in which it was too close to something I couldn't name or bear to constantly relive for the next forty years.

I don't know many people here. I spend the first few weeks couch-surfing, because my living arrangements have fallen through catastrophically. I make one resident friend in the first few weeks, Todd, who is from the West Coast and critiques everything I wear. He has come up with a motivational mantra he chants into my voicemail every time I don't pick up the phone: *Our lives suck.*

Residency is really tough—terrifying, actually. I'm rotating through a lineup of massive downtown teaching hospitals, each one bigger than the next. At Mac, people were pretty calm. My new colleagues seem like they're on amphetamines.

We start our days with an exercise in humiliation and dominance: morning report. At my first new hospital, this standard-practice spectacle is led by an old Dutch physician lauded by the local internal medicine residents as an institution. He sits at the head of a huge oblong table. The chief resident begins by telling the Dutchman about a challenging or interesting case on the internal medicine service. Then the Dutchman, beginning with the student on either his left or right, asks questions about the case. So, if you sit next to him on his right, you have a 50 percent chance of getting his first question, which will usually be fairly basic—in which case, you'll probably be spared looking like a fool. But if he starts on the opposite side, you have a 50 percent chance of getting one of the questions that comes after he has worked his way around the table—and those questions are likely to be incredibly specific. If you're unlucky enough be on the wrong side of that table, and the Dutchman asks you a question that you not only can't answer but might never be able to answer because it is so esoteric and abstract, a long, ominous pause will ensue. That silence speaks for itself. It tells everybody in the room what you really are: an imposter.

Is it any wonder that one day, sitting in those rounds, I have a stomachache? And then again the day after that? The free muffins and coffee and fruit, all laid out like a recurring last meal:

none of them tempt me. Day by day, I get more nauseated. I'm doing a thirty-hour in-hospital call shift one-in-four—every fourth night—and when I'm not on call, I'm so wired from residual adrenalin I can barely sleep. Patients here are really, really sick. The other night somebody bled to death in front of me, a column of red spurting out of their mouth like Old Faithful. The ward is my personal version of Vietnam, and I don't know who to talk to about it. I can't worry my family. I don't have friends here yet besides Todd. And I'm not about to risk making any of the faculty think I can't handle the pressure.

So one day, in the hall, because I don't even have a family doctor and I think maybe I have an ulcer, I timidly ask the Dutchman if he could see me. He tells me to come by his office the next day. His nurse ushers me in. I put on a paper gown for the exam. The Dutchman asks me some questions. He pokes at my abdomen. He says kindly that everything looks good, and I'm probably just buckling under stress. He tells me if I lost ten pounds, my weight would be perfect for my height. Then he says something about family medicine residency being very stressful, and when I correct him and say I am an internal medicine resident, I'm fairly sure his face registers surprise.

Why would he be surprised? The answer comes to me as I'm shedding the stupid paper gown and slipping back into my clothes. He is surprised because internal medicine residents usually know more in internal medicine rounds than family medicine residents, and he's remembering my silence around the table. I'm *sure* of it. He's seen right through me; he knows the truth about me. I don't belong here, the home of the discovery of insulin, walking in the shadows of Banting and Best. I'm not one of the best. I'm the idiot who can't even remember how to write an order for an insulin infusion or peritoneal dialysis, the same one who panicked last week and blurted out something about a fire ant when the Dutchman was going around the table, asking us for increasingly obscure differential diagnoses of a kind of skin lesion I couldn't even pronounce. One summer I learned half of Bach's Goldberg Variations by memory in less than seven days, the next half the following week. Every note, thousands of them, by memory. There's no way any of the people at the rounds table could do that. There's no way the *Dutchman* could do that. But now, I'm the girl who can't even remember where the nurses keep the tongue depressors, no matter how many times they show me. And all I can see is the look on the Dutchman's face, my memory of his expression more incredulous and further from reality each time I recall it.

Thereafter, in morning report, I developed a kind of neurotic feedback loop. No matter where I was seated at the table, I would think to myself, *I'm not going to know the answer*. It became impossible to muffle that screaming, accusatory voice, even though on the wards I actually seemed to be taking pretty decent care of patients and had kind of figured out what to do when someone was having chest pain or seizing or just needed a few kind words in moments of pain or existential crisis. At McMaster, I was relaxed, invigorated and valedictorian; the residents had called me "super-clerk." Even when I was tired and post-call, I still radiated an inner joy and confidence, a feeling of being among my people and doing something I wanted and needed to do.

But something had snuffed out that light. The tree the Dutchman had unwittingly planted was a barbed, poisonous invader. I lost confidence. I perseverated. I couldn't shut off an alarm that was sounding constantly, telling me London was burning. The Dutchman said there was nothing the matter with me, but I had a problem that was about to take a much more serious turn.

Camus knew when he wrote *The Nausea* that it wasn't just a physical symptom but rather a state of mind—a deep affliction, both emotional and physical. I began to suffer nausea from the time I woke up in the morning to the time I lay down for bed. I tried manipulating my diet. I cut out dairy, then gluten, even before gluten was declared an enemy of the people. I boiled ginger root and drank it as an elixir. I tried acupuncture on myself with a small-gauge IV needle, so my arm looked like I really had been bitten by a fire ant. I took Gravol, rendering me barely able to stay awake during even the regular twelve-hour days, let alone the ones that spilled over to thirty. I tried eating less. Then less still. And then, by accident, I discovered that I am one of those people who feels excellent when I eat very little, and that I feel even more excellent when I eat almost nothing—all the inconvenience, light-headedness, obsessiveness and unnatural weirdness associated with eating next to nothing outweighed by the total relief of low-grade starvation-induced chemical euphoria. Somewhere, in the back of my mind, I must have remembered that the Dutchman had given me a hint. There was at least one way I could be perfect.

That was my emergency switch. I had only been a doctor for six months when I discovered it. Soon I was hitting that switch literally all the time. On call? Don't eat anything. Home alone and worried about tomorrow's exam? Bed without dinner will take care of that. The need for relief got bigger, I got smaller, and soon the whole thing had evolved into a situation I couldn't really recognize, because I was walking around in a state of semi-starvation, looking more like a coked-out Ralph Lauren model than a person who should be running cardiac arrests at one of the biggest hospitals in Canada.

I read about this all the time, and you probably do too. Women and the odd gay or straight man, often artists, sometimes academics, interviewed about their most difficult years, saying something coy, like "I was taking terrible care of myself. I'd drink coffee and eat a stick of Juicy Fruit, then go to the gym for three hours." Sweethearts, that's not just taking terrible care of yourself; that's an eating disorder. Somewhere in the next paragraph, a nod to the current state, which involves being a suspiciously angular yoga instructor/keto-vegan/Iron Man or Woman. This is gaslighting. It's scattered throughout all age groups and professions, a tweetable insta-scam.

Occasionally, during my years as associate dean, a student would come into my office, rail thin, mood a little too elevated, with a too-bright smile, yet bringing a shadow into the room. I'd know that shadow anywhere. I'd feel a tightness in my chest as I watched her contort her body in the chair across from me, could almost inhabit her rising panic about jeans too tight, hip bones not palpable enough beneath what she was convinced was a thick layer of subcutaneous fat. She had painted herself into the corner of the attic, and now had to choose. Stay put, or ruin the masterpiece.

Looking back through the prism of the curse of knowledge, I was such an excellent candidate for an eating disorder. The only remarkable thing is that it emerged so late. The tendency to play the piano until I couldn't feel my fingers. The desire to always do my part, to never give anybody anything to worry about. The inability to label situations correctly, or my own feelings correctly, because my own feelings had to be carefully managed, contained, needed their own handler. I could look almost anybody in the eye and say I was perfectly fine in a withering voice that made them feel stupid for even asking. My residency was drilling into me that the needs of every single person in the hospital were more important than mine. I would do anything for anyone; the worse their circumstances, the more I rose to the occasion. But the one person I seemed totally unwilling to help was myself.

Why was that so difficult for me? The literature tells us that siblings of children with disabilities often experience lasting challenges of their own. There's a storybook version of that life, one I used to tell every time someone handed me a microphone. *My sister's my hero. My parents are my heroes. I'm so lucky my siblings are disabled, because it made me who I am.* There's a current of truth in that version, an alternate, more meaningful life of service I get to live as a result of those things, different than the life I might have had without it, a way in which we are christened in flames. But good/bad or blessing/curse is hardly the whole story. I was a classic dichotomous thinker, another thing that made me a top-tier candidate for a top-tier eating disorder.

What might my residency, my life, have been like without the full-time job of hiding a secret vice? Why, instead of walking past the eating disorders clinic, cowering behind the ID badge that said I was a doctor, didn't I walk right in? Part of the illness is you don't believe it's an illness at all. No matter how many warning lights are blinking, you don't see a problem. You don't open your mail for months. Then one day, your heat goes off, but you never make a connection between these things. That's what it was like for me. I couldn't see why I needed to cross into that waiting room, couldn't think of a reason why this problem was even a problem, or why it would be worthy of anyone's attention.

How did I get over it? There were fits and starts, flares and times when it faded into silence because other things drowned it out, and eventually, down the road, a psychiatrist who listened for long enough to ask the right questions, the ones I'd been avoiding for most of my life, and helped me find the right answers. It still flares sometimes, very occasionally, the way a bum knee acts up when you push it too far. I've retreated to it during times of total emotional overload, just the way you might go back to a bad relationship in a moment of extreme vulnerability. But I'm mostly done with it, and vice versa. I like euphemisms; I like saying I struggled. But what I was really struggling with was a void in my life, a pre-existing hole that the soul-crushing aspects of being a doctor continued to probe and excavate for years. All these things were related. One devil hand-feeding another.

Early on, there was one epiphany. In the years that followed I would come back to it, examining it from different angles the way you inspect something you've had for a long time when you're trying to decide whether it is worth keeping. It came like a vision, a few years into the whole mess. I was post-call, walking home through a park. I stopped suddenly in the middle of a rundown playground, sat on the edge of a rusty slide. I saw it so clearly in that moment. All the starving and exercising, obsessing and organizing my life around food: none of that was going to change anything. It was all just palliation, self-medicating, like numbing pain with booze or drugs. None of it would restore my sister to her former glory; none of it would put the piece back into my family's life that was obliterated before I was even born, and none of it would change one bloody thing. I glimpsed the truth in that moment, but I wasn't ready to let that truth into my life. And I wish things hadn't gone on for so long, or gotten quite so out of control, because I don't get to go back and do another take of those prime years of my life when I was renting out a lot of my best cognitive real estate to a tenant I didn't know how to evict.

My dad used to say, you can't turn back the clock, not even one second. When I was growing up, it had always seemed like a platitude. But I would come to see it as a sacred truth, a simple truth that can take us our whole life to apprehend: we are never, ever going back.

o o o

RIGHT AT THE start of this madness, in the first several weeks of my residency when I felt I was just barely keeping my head above water, my staff physician stopped me on the ward and asked if we could meet later that afternoon. He wanted to give me some feedback about my performance on the rotation thus far. I went through the next few hours in a daze, staring at blank pages in charts I was supposed to be filling with notes. *He's figured out I don't know anything*, I thought miserably. *He knows I'm an imposter.* I tried to think of what I'd say, how I'd justify my performance, whether it was still possible for me to salvage my career. How would I tell my parents? I had loans to pay. I'd never get another full scholarship to Oxford. I had come so far, all of it for nothing.

I was practically trembling when I went to his office, knocked timidly on the door, sat down, my gaze settled on the floor. My eyes were seconds away from filling with tears as I awaited the inevitable blow. He knew the truth about me; I would confess to it all. I opened my mouth to apologize. *Mea culpa.*

Before I could say anything, he clapped me enthusiastically

on the shoulder. "First month is almost over, and things are going great!"

There was a long pause.

"They are?" I said quietly.

"You're a star, Jillian. You're chief resident material."

I remember his outline was blurry, my eyes barely able to focus because I was so sleep-deprived. I blinked several times, the way people do when they are going under anesthetic, catching a last glimpse of the world for what could turn out to be a very long time.

It would be years before I understood the profound lesson of that moment: doing a good job, and knowing you have done a good job, are two separate skills.

I only had one of them.

9

Answers Don't Change

We line up for breakfast in the kitchen. There's a huge, comical vat of oatmeal. A pineapple and a watermelon, dissected. Boiled eggs. Bread and jam and a pillar of pats of butter. Pots and pots of coffee.

The windows in the dining hall look out onto the stream and the old mill. There's a hint of frost visible on the grass, the light around the trees still baby pink. Greg is behind me in the food line.

"Hey, sorry for running into you."

"No problem. Woke me up."

"Thanks for not suing."

"I didn't agree to that." He uses tongs to wrangle an egg onto his plate. I pretend not to see when the egg slips and rolls under one of the kitchen cabinets. He takes another one.

I fill a bowl with oatmeal. The kitchen smells like holiday: cinnamon and oranges. Jodie waves at me from across the line. I point the oatmeal ladle at her like a weapon and glare.

"I'm guessing you're not a surgeon?" I say to Greg.

He pours cream over his oatmeal, dousing it with brown sugar. "Or diabetic?"

Jodie calls over: "Is she bothering you?"

"All under control. I'm an ER doc."

I hand him some cutlery. "I guessed that."

"Why?"

We head to an empty table in a corner by the window, set our plates down.

"You seem kind of unflappable."

"I just do my flapping on the inside."

"Doesn't that sound like one of those consults that makes you want to kill yourself?"

"Or somebody else."

"Totally." I watch him take a sip of coffee. He cuts his egg in half, revealing a neon yolk.

"So why are you here?" I ask him.

He doesn't answer right away. "I should know this, right? I had lots of time to rehearse last night." He takes another sip of coffee.

"Ok, so, Greg, I was buying a futon once when I was a student. I kept going to look at all the options. I guess I went into the same store twice by accident, and I asked the guy how much for a queen futon. And he points his finger at me and says, 'You've been here before! Answers don't change!'"

"But answers *do* change."

"Or do questions change? Or does honesty change?"

"This would be the line of questioning in a more existential futon store."

"Yes! Like, 'What is sleep but non-awakening?'"

"I remember when I was a resident." He shakes his head wist-

72

fully. "I was always thinking how when I was done, I was going to get the best mattress money could buy, and blackout curtains so I'd feel like I was in outer space."

"I had that same obsession with perfect sleep. Like it was a narcotic."

"And meanwhile I'm still hitting the hay on a twenty-year-old piece of junk from Sears."

"Why didn't you buy that dream bed?"

"Don't know." He eats the rest of his egg. The sugar has mottled the surface of his oatmeal, like a bruise.

"Greg, it's melodrama, but do you think it's like, it never really ended? You're back home, but it still looks identical to the frontline. Why bother changing anything if you're still at war?"

He nods. "Nail on the head."

"Now there's a classic ER problem."

Jodie slips into an empty seat next to us.

"Pretty sure that's a nail *in* the head. Greg, have you met Jodie?"

They shake hands. Greg shows her his nametag. Then he looks puzzled. "How do you two know each other if Jill's from Canada?"

"Past life."

Jodie is still wearing her meditation shawl. She has it folded around her neck in a complex configuration, like a piece of origami. "How did you guys like Zendo?"

"I thought it was a Game of Thrones kind of thing. I tried to take Greg out."

"She did."

Jodie pulls out the blue folder of information we all received when we checked in. "We're all in an Affinity group together."

"Well, whatever that is, at least we're not going to spoil three groups."

Greg looks skeptical. "Isn't that a presumptuous name? What if we hate each other?"

Jodie raises her coffee mug as if proposing a toast. "Then we can call it an *Infinity* group."

He clinks his cup against hers. "'Cause that's what it will feel like!"

The hall is full now. There's a happy, camp-like din. Conversation, laughter, noise from cutlery and dishes. People are wearing T-shirts and sweatpants, moccasins and slippers. You'd never guess this was a group of doctors. We look like we're being prepped to reintegrate into society.

In fact, we aren't actually part of normal society, not anymore. Medicine does something to us. It teaches us another language, one only other doctors can understand. Eventually it scripts our emotions, neutralizing them whenever they threaten to overwhelm the senses. This also happens to police and firefighters, coroners and soldiers and paramedics, a misguided *Clockwork Orange* rewiring of the motherboard. But it's not by accident.

Once, when a friend of mine was a resident in the intensive care unit, she was looking after a young woman who had a sudden, catastrophic bleed into her brain. Two little children were crawling on their mother's motionless body, her brain in her skull liquefied by the pressure of blood with nowhere to go, tissue turned to mush, like an overripe banana. The youngest one kept saying, *Wake up, Mommy. Mommy, it's morning. It's time to wake up.* My colleague, doing a neurologic exam, checking for reflexes, prying open the woman's eyelids to see massive, unresponsive pupils, black as oil, big and round like pennies. All the while, that little child was slapping her mother's cheeks, pinching fingernails that still bore the jovial, piglet pink of what looked like a fresh manicure. Those *nails*. That was the thing that got her, just as much as the soon-to-be orphaned child. My colleague stepped out of the room and ducked into a storage area a few doors down, stifling a sob she'd only just barely been suppressing. She heard footsteps. The staff physician appeared and stood in the doorway. He looked at her, his face as expressionless as that of a corpse in the anatomy lab. He said: "This is an emotion-free zone." He walked away.

"Do you guys know if Mick writes all his own poetry?"

Jodie looks at me over the top of her bifocals. "Mick writes poetry?"

"What he read in the Zendo." I feel my cheeks flush. "Wasn't that his?"

She giggles. "That's David Whyte. Probably just the best-known living Buddhist poet in the Western world."

"Hey, no way," says Greg. "That's Mary Oliver."

"I didn't know she was a Buddhist."

Jodie laughs through a mouthful of coffee, accidentally spitting some in my direction.

"Gross, Jodie."

She wipes coffee off her chin. "Jill doesn't speak American. We'd better explain everything."

"Look, morons, is she really a Buddhist?"

Greg waves his index finger at me. "Answers don't change!"

Jodie leans in and whispers, "Can you imagine the three of us working together?"

"More like *not* working."

"Where do I sign?" says Greg.

Little Green Shoot

N oticing the breath.

Breath is a vital sign. I was trained to notice other people's breath. I notice if they're breathing too fast or slow. It's often one of the earliest, subtlest clues that something is changing. A pneumonia is getting worse. Heart failure is brewing. Acid is slowly building up in the body and the lungs are working overtime to spew it out as carbon dioxide. If you're going to avoid killing people, you learn to treat the breath with respect.

But nobody ever instructed me to notice my own breath. I've noticed it before, but just barely. Like when you're looking at a tree and suddenly discern a bird, hidden among the leaves. Or when you're sitting on a beach, staring out at the water, and suddenly you really see the way the light dances on it, splintered into diamond ridges.

We split from our bodies so we can learn to be doctors. Isn't that ironic? We deal with corporeal failures, but we think we can program bodies, *our* bodies, to run without sleep, or food, or hydration. We learn to work through utter exhaustion. We dismantle the safety valves evolution built to keep us from doing anything important or dangerous on too little sleep. When our ancestors were apes, was it good for them to be out in the dark gathering bananas? No, they were better off in their ape beds, where they wouldn't stumble over cliffs in the pitch black. Medical education says: You know why that ancestor of yours needed sleep? Because he was an ape. And by extension, if you can't function without sleep, well, that can only mean you're an ape too.

The hilarious thing is that in recent years, medical organizations have begun using the same wellness buzzwords as everybody else, telling us to practise self-care. How can *I* practise self-care? My training was an apprenticeship in the art of self-immolation. I excelled at it; I strove to master it the same way I applied my full self to everything. You don't just undo that overnight. If you ever undo it at all.

Why didn't we question it? We didn't even have a language to describe what we would have been questioning. Words like *burn-out* were reserved for people who were so ill they couldn't work. Those people existed on the periphery of our consciousness, vanishing on personal leaves or mysterious, non-existent "research" blocks, because they were afraid to tell anybody what was really going on. We never knew what force was quietly picking off the people around us. We thought that kind of attrition was normal. And so, we experienced a slow drift away from normalcy, the tether giving way over not months but years.

Once, when I was an intern, I was rounding, and on my twenty-eighth hour with no sleep, listening to the attending physician ramble about examining a patient's spleen, while we interns, all post-call, tried to stay upright around the bed. A wall of intense nausea dropped in front of me like a curtain. I stepped out of the room and into the closet-like bathroom reserved for the nurses, where I threw up the little food I'd eaten the night before, then bright green bile. I paused, rinsed my mouth with tap water, and rejoined the others a few rooms down. I was gone for less than two minutes. The attending physician was still talking about the spleen. He hadn't even noticed I was gone.

Pride. That's what I felt then. Pride at my own ability to take blows as they came, pride that I could suffer so secretly, so completely, while standing shoulder-to-shoulder with these men. Pride, too, the following year: sick with another virus in the middle of a call shift, vomiting so forcefully that I bled behind the white of one eye, but still staying on, shivering in the glassed-in fishbowl internal medicine room in the emergency department, still reviewing cases with the juniors. Pride, the next morning, not in the emergency department but in the call room, when one of the more senior residents slipped an IV into a collapsed vein on the back of my hand and squeezed in a bag of normal saline, both of us laughing like it was just a big joke. *"You okay to get home on your own?"* *"Oh please, it's just a gastro for fuck's sake."* Pride, despite the utter self-neglect, the incredible, shocking stupidity of this on both sides.

I flag that first day on rounds as one more stop on a long journey towards abandoning myself to a deep and smoke-like darkness that permeated everything, sowing the seed of a problem that grew deep, deep roots.

You can mostly convince yourself that whatever you're inflicting in that darkness, whether it's an eating disorder or just quietly failing to provide yourself with the emotional and physical necessities of life, at least it's not like you're buying drugs on the street. You're not going to be found blue, pulseless, overdosed with a needle in your arm somewhere in a seedy hotel.

But it is still a way you kill yourself. Not necessarily the body, but the literal, precious self, the best part of you: the part of you that is real and authentic, the part that loves, deeply. That part can die. That part is a little green shoot. I thought it was supposed to take care of me, not the other way around. If I didn't water that shoot for years, how did it survive? Or did it?

Mick, I'm noticing my thoughts.

I'm noticing my thoughts are very dark.

Things in Boxes

Our Affinity group meets in the Zendo. Me, Greg, Jodie and a woman named Joss who looks to be the same age as me but is, damn her, a lot thinner.

I said I was *mostly* over it.

The bell rings in the main hall, our cue to begin. We're studying a poem, doing something called "close reading."

This feels flaky.

Jodie sighs. "I'll read. One for the team."

Grace

Those first few weeks were agony. July
Sweated me into stupor. The ink not dry on my degree.
The angels must have thought I was a dunce.
I sat in chapels crying more than once.

That maze of halls I barely knew, those wards
My family a thousand miles away
My things all still in boxes, as a day
To take them out eluded me. It's hard.

It's hard. Two words we never say enough
To anyone. We're rude, or gruff, or, worse still,
Silent. We seldom know the grace
Of love we stubbornly rebuff.

We sit looking at each other.

"Should we read it again?"

"I will. Jodie's done her civic duty."

Joss reads the poem a second time. There's a long pause.

Greg clears his throat. "I'm kind of drawn to the way she uses religious imagery. You know, the . . ." He pauses, scanning the poem again. "The 'chapel.' The 'angels.' The 'grace of love.'"

Greg, I'm kind of drawn to you, actually. Nothing seedy, totally platonic. You just have this presence, this energy that makes me want to sit and talk to you all morning. You're someone I'd share jokes and meaningful glances with if we worked together in the emergency department. But I'd never guess that you're flapping on the inside. Seriously, why are *you* here?

"I'm just getting a feeling of this deep loneliness, actually," Jodie says.

Jodie, I'm drawn to you too. You're another person I could go for a long coffee with every month for the rest of my life. Someone I'd like for a sister or an aunt.

The group is looking at me.

"Am I the only person here who feels like a moron? Seriously,

I mean, I have a degree in English, but I feel like a fucking idiot doing this. Sorry, can I swear here?"

Jodie rolls her eyes. "No judgment."

Joss says, "Fuck yeah."

"Now I'm at home."

"Is it Zen to swear?"

"If it's done with awareness."

"We should still talk about the poem."

"Yeah, let's talk about the effing poem."

"Guys, the other line that jumps out at me is, '*my things in boxes.*'" God, Greg's just so achingly *earnest.* How hard he's trying is seriously breaking my heart.

"What do you think that's about?"

"Well, we shove everything down, right? I mean, I assume this poem is about residency. It's taken me almost thirty years to unpack all that, and I'm still not done."

Jodie says, "Nobody knows that about us."

"I feel like we all have one of those boxes." Joss has straight blond hair and an outrageously excellent vintage necklace set with turquoise and mother-of-pearl. "I'm afraid to even look at what's still in mine."

"Like whatever's in there might just jump out at you and eat your face."

"Like it *did* eat my face. Or maybe what's in the box is what used to be my face."

"Do any of you guys ever feel like you're the last person anyone expects to feel that way?

"Jodie, you've been silent for more than thirty seconds. Are you okay?"

"Now it's *An*imosity group."

Greg keeps us on track. "Hey, so what's the bit about 'rude, or gruff, or worse still silent'?"

"Don't you think that's how we treat each other?"

"Some departments consider being a dick a core competency."

"In Canada? You've got to be kidding." Jodie shuts her eyes, puts the back of her hand against her forehead and pretends to faint.

It's funny. I throw a cushion at her.

"Were you both, like, the bad kids in medical school?"

"Who said we went to medical school?"

"Animosity group," says Joss. "Let's hear this puppy one more time."

She reads the poem again.

We're all quiet for a minute.

"That was a totally different poem. I heard some of that for the first time."

"It's kind of like, just *validate* this, right? It's fucking *hard*."

Joss pauses, clears her throat. "You want to know what's really in my unpacked box?"

This time nobody makes a joke. Joss takes a long, deep breath. Her voice is quiet. "Have you guys ever treated near-drowning?"

I have. But long after the fact, only in the ICU. The others are shaking their heads, no.

"I looked after a kid once, in Pediatrics. Fell through the ice. It was just . . ." Joss pauses, takes off her glasses, cleans them on the tail of her shirt. "She was so cold it hurt my hands to touch her. Like, we couldn't even draw blood."

"How old?"

"Seven."

"God."

"Ice in her mouth. Like slush when we did chest compressions. Like a slushie, basically."

"Oh fuck." Jodie has her hand over her mouth. "I take it she died?"

"It was hopeless." Joss is tearing up. "I actually wrote a poem about it, but I can't remember how it goes. It was terrible."

"It sounds ghastly," says Greg.

She corrects him. "I mean the poem was terrible." She fishes in her pocket for a tissue. "But yes, the case was ghastly. One of my top ten worst cases of all time. Mother screaming in the waiting room. Younger sister who'd been with her." She blows her nose. "They were sledding."

Jodie lets out a low whistle.

Joss wipes her eyes and points at the clock on the wall. "Thank you, Insanity group." She blows her nose again. "Wasn't expecting that."

Jodie gives her a hug. "Never are."

12

Christmas Is Coming

Noticing.

Ron has a picture up on the screen. An explosion. A bunch of farmhouses.

"Tell me what you see." Mick walks around with the microphone. People are putting up their hands.

"Crystal-blue sky."

"Grey stone." *Those are mountains.*

"Some kind of dark . . . puffy substance on top of it."

That's smoke. You all know it's an explosion. Call it a bloody explosion.

"A building in the distance."

I know it's a building in the distance. Could we stop the days-of-wonder thing?

"Anything else?" Mick asks.

"Maybe an . . . explosion?"

Mick presses the woman who spoke. "What makes you say it's an explosion?"

Nothing, Mick. Everything is perfectly fine. Wait, is that a crowd of people running for their lives?

"Light on the windows?" someone says. A woman, maybe my age.

She's right . . . a part of the row of windows on a farmhouse is illuminated in a straight line, a spear of pure light.

So what.

People keep chiming in. Don't they feel the least bit self-conscious? Some of them are falling over themselves to sound clever. This is kind of an affront to my intellect.

"There's a . . . modern building in the distance." Jodie.

Excuse me, sister, but don't you also think this is ridiculous? I thought I had your number.

Somebody says the scene is of a tornado. Or a fire burning. There's discussion about this.

Ron points out how we go to interpreting right away, that we're scrambling for an explanation before we've even noticed what we're looking at. It's Iceland, he adds, in 2012. A farmer woke up one day to find that a volcano he'd looked at every day for the last sixty years had blown.

"Same thing happens with an aorta," says one of the surgeons. The group laughs.

Then Ron plays a video of people playing basketball. He asks us to count how many passes the players on the red team make. I watch, grudgingly. I count eight.

Then he asks: "Who saw the moonwalking bear?"

Oh, fuck off, Ron.

Except then he replays the video, and there really is a moon-walking bear.* It shuffles right through the circle of basketball players.

Okay, that was odd.

He shows us a CT scan of the chest and asks us what we see. It's up on the screen, a section of the midlung.

He asks for the diagnosis. Some people notice a nodule. Maybe a pericardial effusion? A rib fracture? There's some disagreement. A radiologist in the group says there's a possibility of lymphangitic carcinomatosis. He gets up and points to a spot with his fingers. Everybody squints. Silence.

Ron asks if anyone noticed the gorilla in the left upper lobe.

He highlights it, with a small purple arrow. It's true. There's a gorilla on the CT scan.

There are fifty physicians in this room. Specialists, generalists, surgeons. Every kind of doctor. We probably have five hundred years of combined post-secondary education.

Not one of us saw a gorilla.[†]

Ron says this is the concept of beginner's mind. Seeing without expectations or interpretations. Seeing with a sense of wonder. Noticing.

He asks us to take a few minutes to do an exercise called "Ten minutes of red."

---

* The "invisible" moonwalking bear video (titled "Awareness Test") was created in 2008 for Transport for London (TfL) as part of a safety campaign, "Look Out for Cyclists." Developed by advertising agency WCRS, it was shown in U.K. cinemas for a week before being released on social media and going viral.

† Results of the "gorilla in the lung" study were reported in 2013 by researchers Trafton Drew and Jeremy Wolfe, and based in part on 1999 studies by Christopher Chabris and Daniel Simon, whose Invisible Gorilla test is still among the best-known demonstrations of "inattentional blindness."

"Walk around the room," he tells us. "Just do it in silence. Take a piece of paper and write down everything you see that's red." The only rule is not to talk.

We take sheets of paper out of our folders. I have a red pen tucked into the side of mine. I take the pen and write down: *red pen*. Underneath that, in tiny letters so no one can read it over my shoulder, I write: *This feels like bullshit.* I take a quick look around. This room is all neutral tones, like you might picture your grandma's condo in the afterlife.

But I get up and, along with everyone else, start circling the perimeter of the hall with my paper and pen.

Fire alarm
Fire bell
Red light on the smoke detector

Exit

Somebody's coffee cup

Somebody's scarf—silk

Rose on windowsill
Four more roses on windowsill
Writing on Greg's shirt
This is stupid

Ron and Mick run a cult

I am noticing I feel totally stupid.

Car lights outside of window
Writing now so I look like I am participating
Person who talks too much—her shoelaces
That girl's necklace
Red on screen

Light from projector
Pool of human blood
Gorilla meditating in corner
Tall guy's sweatpants
Thing with Buddha on it
Buddha's wiener under his diaper
Clock rim
Kool-Aid

Writing on emergency preparedness sign

Ron rings his bell. We sit back down. He asks what that was like. Somebody I haven't met yet, an Asian woman about the same age as me, says, "At first I thought there was nothing red in here. Then I could only see red."

The man who made the aorta joke: "I wanted to get the most red. I wanted to kick your asses." Everybody laughs.

Greg puts up his hand. "I was annoyed. It felt infantile. Then I noticed that I was annoyed. All this chatter was going on in my head while I was doing a mundane task. I was making it harder for myself by resisting what I had to do."

Ah, resisting. There we go. Bring on the Kool-Aid.

Ron asks if that made it harder to focus. A bunch of people nod.

Jodie calls out: "Plus I found myself wondering, what's red, anyway?"

"This pissed me off," I whisper to her.

She waves at Mick, points at me. I elbow her in the ribs but it's too late . . . he's already handed me the mic.

"I found that I was, um, annoyed that you were trying to make me do this."

"Ah!" says Ron. Now he's smiling. "Say more about that?"

"Well, um." I fiddle with the microphone for a second. "Just that I think I did a worse job because I thought, *I'll show him, I'll just notice a few things that are red.*"

Everybody laughs again. Did I mean for that to be funny?

"And do you feel like you showed me?"

"I'm pretty sure it was the other way around." More laughter. I hand the microphone back to Mick, glowering at Jodie.

"The point here is that you can notice more than one thing. You can notice external stimuli and internal stimuli at the same time. You can also notice where you draw a line. Like Jodie said, What's red? What if you're tired? What if you're well-slept? What if you're not looking for red? What if you *are* looking for red?"

I look down at the list in my lap. Was I looking for red?

Maybe I'm here because I don't see any colours anymore, Ron. I'm here because I'm having my own quiet emergency, and if anyone were looking for it, they'd see it too. But they don't know what they're looking for, just like I didn't know to look for the moonwalking bear or the gorilla or the flashes of red in this eggshell room. All those times during residency when I was stumbling around the hospital like Edvard Munch's *The Scream* come to life. I wasn't just struggling, I was disappearing into a sinkhole. I remember thinking, *How come nobody knows?* And then, more ominously, *Obviously they don't care.*

Doctors have the highest suicide rate of any white-collar profession. Why exactly is that?

Ron is saying to find a partner. I don't know if I'm up for this. It feels so syrupy to me, like next he's going to whip out old magazines and assign a difficult feelings collage. If this gets too weird, I'll ditch this place.

Except where would I go? Into the woods? Cram myself under a toadstool somewhere and wait for the shuttle to come back at the end of the week? I feel a flicker of something again, the spectre of a deep gash of hurt. The other doctors look like they're participating. They're not writing *Buddha's wiener* on their list of red objects.

I guess I look like I'm participating too. And I don't know what's on other people's lists; you never really know what anyone else is thinking. Intellectually, I can see every point Ron is making, can understand how each of them apply to me. I'm not a lost cause. Maybe he and Mick are offering me something here. Do I want to take it? Christ, it's not lithium.

I catch Greg's eye. *Go together?*

He nods.

The group breaks up into pairs. I move over to Greg. We met yesterday, but there's an intimacy between us, a lack of pretense. Maybe even a sense of urgency, because we like each other and there's not much time. I think we might have the same set point, the same baseline levels of cynicism and vulnerability.

Ron projects instructions up onto the screen.

Think of a time at work when you made a difference or something went well. Notice what you find yourself thinking about as you write. Notice the associated feelings and whatever was going through your mind at the time. Write it down, then share it with your partner.

93

"I don't do anything well," Greg whispers before we start writing.

A Time I Did Something Well at Work
Although the story begins with me doing something really badly

By Jill H.

This was early in my career. I had just moved back to the prairies. At least half my patients were from the reserves. They had the shittiest lives you could imagine. No running water. Mould-infested houses. Third-world conditions. Child poverty and kids dying from totally preventable infectious disease. Ongoing trauma from the separation of families, the legacy of residential schools and cultural genocide. I thought I knew all this. I thought it was terrible and unacceptable. So I didn't think I was racist.

Mr. Raven had been in the hospital for a week when I took over his care. His family was all still up north. He was hard-living and hard-drinking. He'd been in and out of jail. Robbery, but never hurt anybody, the social worker said. It was just to get liquor. Always things he did when he was drunk. His liver was failing from booze, and he was constantly vomiting up blood. I went to say hello to him, and he told me to go away. I didn't mind, because I had a lot of other things to do. I guess if I'm being honest, I was glad he let me off the hook.

He swore a lot at the residents and nurses. I got calls that he was refusing bloodwork, refusing to let the nurses change his IVs. But one morning the ward paged me to say that his hemoglobin was 55—lower than usual. He needed more blood. I called the nurse and ordered it. She paged me back a half-hour later.

94

"Mr. Raven said we can all fuck off and that he doesn't want any fucking blood." Her voice was full of disgust. "If you want him to have blood, you're going to have to talk to him."

I sighed. I'd been called a bunch of times overnight about sick patients, urgent lab reports, a patient who left against medical advice. I was tired, and already behind in admitting people from the emergency department. I went up to the ward, where I found Mr. Raven in bed in his room, flannel blanket pulled up almost to his forehead, as if he were a dead man waiting for the porter to shuttle him to the morgue.

"Mr. Raven," I said, "I heard you told the nurses to fuck off. It's not okay to talk to them like that. We're just trying to help you. We need to give you blood."

There was no movement under the sheet. "Mr. Raven?" I said again. I was exasperated. There was a long pause. I could just write in the chart that he was refusing blood. That would be enough to absolve me of responsibility if he bled to death. You can't force treatment on people. They have choices.

Was he asleep? My pager was going off again. He curled up under the blanket, kicked his leg like a swaddled baby. I didn't have time for this.

"Mr. Raven," I said impatiently, "are you going to talk to me at all? Will you let us help you or not?"

I heard a muffled sound coming out from under his pillow. He was crying. It had never occurred to me that he might be crying.

"Mr. Raven?" I said again, but this time I spoke softly, and it was a question instead of a command.

"Nobody tells me anything." His words were muffled beneath the blanket. "Nobody tells me anything that's going on,

95

just uses me as a pincushion. You never even told me why I need that blood."

I stood there for another moment. I hadn't talked to him about his condition. I assumed my colleagues had. But it was totally plausible that nobody had, that each person had found him curled up, or heard that he always swore at the nurses and decided that a conversation was going to take too long and was ultimately a waste of their time. So maybe no one had ever come into that room and pulled up a chair and told him what was happening with his liver. Maybe he'd never asked for it. But why was that incumbent on him? And if the white doctor who can't possibly imagine the shit you've had to deal with in your life is just going to come and stand by your bed with her arms crossed and see you as a criminal and a drunk and give you a tongue-lashing for swearing at the nurses, why would you ask for anything?

I pulled up a chair. I sat down. I leaned towards him. I took his hand. "You're completely right," I said. "I'm so sorry."

We were both silent for a minute. Then his eyes overflowed with even more tears, all the grief he'd been holding in for God knows how long.

"I'm stuck here like I'm in prison. It's so far from home." He took a long, deep breath in, choking on a sob. "And Christmas is coming, eh?"

Christmas is coming. Mr. Raven and Christmas. Mr. Raven wanted to celebrate Christmas with his *family.* How embarrassing, how humbling, how horrifying for me to see that I'd never put those words or concepts together. And I'd made an even bigger mistake than that. I hadn't known he wanted the same things as me. I hadn't known he was the same as me. He loved his family, the same way I did. He had struggled with an addiction, and truthfully, albeit in a different way, I had too. I had just been luckier—so much luckier. No matter how difficult things had been for me growing up, my family and I always had each other. We always knew there was love. And while we had to deal with discrimination against my sister, none of it was ever because of the colour of our skin. My family had been written off and failed by the medical system. But the same government that had wanted my parents to throw my sister into a glorified dog kennel had done that very thing to Mr. Raven's people. They had stolen everything from him. And here I was, the very person who should know better, failing him.

Mr. Raven and I talked for a long time that day. I held his hand. I told him again I was sorry, that he was absolutely right, that he had taught me something important about racism and how easy it was to make assumptions about other people. I told him I'd work very hard to never do that again. I told him every-thing I could about his condition, in as much detail as possible. I asked him to tell me about his family, his children, what else I could do to make his life better while he was in the hospi-tal. I came back the next day, and the next. He said he liked basketball. I brought him a stack of copies of *Sports Illustrated*. I brought him some new track pants and a toothbrush and a couple of shirts that fit over his distended, fluid-filled belly. Each day I sat, and talked to him, and he let me give him blood transfusions, and he started taking his medicines when the nurse brought them, because now somebody had actually explained what they were for.

A couple of days before Christmas, he was finally ready to go home. We had arranged a night at the boarding home, then a ride up north. I needed to give him his prescriptions. He was waiting for me at the front desk. He put his hand out for me to shake, and his eyes were yellow but his gaze clear and penetrating.

I asked if I could give him a hug. He said yes. I saw how surprised the nurses were as we embraced in the hall.

"Thanks, so much, Jillian," he said shyly. "You're a really good doctor."

There was something so intimate, so lovely about hearing him say my name in that moment. *Jillian*. I didn't know he had noticed. A few days later, on Christmas morning, I thought again about him saying my name. I was glad we had both made it home.

I read Greg what I wrote.

He shakes his head. "Wow."

Ron has put up a slide with more instructions, prompting us to ask specific questions.

Greg peers at the screen through his bifocals. "So . . . what was it about you that let you do that for him?"

"What, give him track pants?"

"Jill," he scolds, "this is a story about seeing somebody as they are. What let you do that?"

"What stopped me from doing that in the first place? Isn't that a better question?"

"Yeah, but that's a different issue. We all have bias. We're racist in ways we don't appreciate without teaching and reflection, right? What about *you* let you put that aside so you could really see him?"

I look down at my paper.

"I don't know, Greg. I don't really think I should be patting myself on the back for seeing a person's humanity."

"Well, maybe you should. I miss people's humanity all the time."

"I doubt that."

"Oh, believe me, I do. In my head I was calling you Smurfette before you sat with me at breakfast."

"I'm an asshole in my head too."

"Seriously, Jill, what let you do that for him? To me it's about meeting a universal human need."

"For track pants?"

He waves his pen at me. "The track pants are a signifier."

"Of what?"

Greg is getting exasperated. "This is *your* story. What do you think the track pants signified?"

"I think they signified that I chose a story that made me look like a hero, when actually I deserved a zero." I draw a big o over everything I've written.

Greg looks over at the instructions again. "I'm . . . curious as to why you think you deserve a zero."

"Because I should have seen his humanity at the start. That's what I'm always beating up other people for."

"Didn't you say this happened years ago? Aren't you allowed to grow?"

"Yes, I'm allowed to grow." I doodle more os around the margins of my story.

Greg points his pen at me in an Uncle-Sam-wants-you gesture. "Then let's try to get real."

"I am real."

"I'm saying it as much for myself as I am for you."

"Okay." I tear the page out of my notebook and crumple up what I've written.

"Why'd you do that?"

"It was lame. I need to get real."

"Okay, well, what would 'getting real' look like to you?"

"No more blue hair."

"Hey, enough." Greg's eyes are stern behind his wire glasses. "What would that look like, Jillian?"

"Well, *Gregory*," I say, and my words hang in the space between us. There's something so endearing about him. He's taking this all so seriously. "For starters, I would not be funny."

"Do you feel like you have to be funny?"

"Sure I do."

"Can you say more about why that is?"

This suddenly feels exhausting, like being in a bad psychiatrist's office.

"I have to make people laugh."

"Why?"

"So they can bear it."

"Bear what?"

"What's coming next."

"And what's coming next?"

"What do you *think* is coming next, Greg?"

His North Face shirt is red. He has a little spider angioma on his neck, red. He makes a slicing motion with his hand across his neck.

"Maybe the guillotine?"

"Bingo!"

Greg pauses. He touches his mouth with the back of his sleeve, as if he has just discovered his lip is bleeding. "I was really young when I started out. I thought anyone could find happiness if they looked hard enough. I had all this idealism, liked my record collection. I thought I was above racism, and bias. I loved John Lennon. He made it seem simple."

"*Jai guru deva.* I totally get that."

"*Om.* Don't you wish something could change our world?"

"Have you ever gone to an AA meeting?"

Greg looks surprised. He hesitates, then tries to sound casual. "No. Have . . . you?"

"No, but a lot of my patients go. You know the first step, right?"

"I don't, actually."

"They start with accepting that life has become unmanageable."

"Well, that's relatable."

"And you have to accept that you're powerless over the thing that's wrecking you."

"I have more trouble with that."

"I don't totally agree with it either, from the perspective of agency. But what if there's something fundamental about how medicine is affecting us that we could fix with a twelve-step program?"

"You mean medicine *is* an addiction?"

"No, I'm not explaining it right. More like the things that help people recover from addiction are the same ones that can help us feel like normal people again."

"Like which things?"

"Well . . . hope. Courage, humility. Love."

Greg is thinking. He milks his little goatee, runs his index finger along his top lip. "But there's this whole separate problem that has nothing to do with us. Medicine is a *business* now. That's the American model, right?"

"It isn't quite so bad in Canada."

"Well, you're lucky. I work for an HMO because they look after all that stuff for me. It isn't necessarily my first choice, but I couldn't deal with insurers on my own. I couldn't run a convenience store. Like, I just want to look after *people*. Is that so much to ask? Not to disrespect the idea of getting more into courage, love, humility . . . whatever you said back there."

"Greg, sometimes this gets so fucking hard, it feels like I'm really looking for a way *out* of medicine."

He nods. "Me too. I feel like Ron and Mick are better people than me."

"Or maybe they're just on better meds."

Greg starts laughing his head off. I get the giggles. Jodie looks over at us from the corner, shakes her head as if we're both lost causes.

"She's jealous!"

We stick our tongues out at her.

"What the hell were we just talking about?"

He shakes his head. "Can't remember. It's too much to keep track of."

"See? Our lives are unmanageable."

"Maybe this *is* a twelve-step program."

"Mick said as much in the Zendo. Remember the first step?"

We share a knowing look. We say it in unison, just as Ron rings that damn bell.

"The step you don't want to take."

The Courtesy Not to Ask

Medicine as a business. Let me share some thoughts on that. In our small prairie town, growing up, we had a family doctor. He's retired now, long since moved. He was a man with admirable qualities, clearly intelligent. He'd gone to school in another country, might have had sherry with tutors. My parents thought he knew a lot, and it was also true that when it came to doctors, they'd seen it all.

He had a busy practice. The clinic in our town served a huge catchment area. As a result, it ran on a care model that would have flummoxed the great medical educator Francis Peabody, who said the secret of caring for the patient is caring for the patient. The clinic flummoxed me too, long before I knew anything about Peabody. Ten minutes per visit, maybe five. And a sign, prominent: *Dr. X is not taking new patients. Please have the courtesy not to ask.*

The courtesy not to *ask.*

The *courtesy* not to ask.

So you start your visit to Dr. X feeling like the clinic has made it abundantly clear to you, in writing, that you're already lucky to be there and they're not interested in people like you taking advantage of their doctor's angelic nature in order to help your family or circle of friends. Then, at least thirty minutes behind schedule, Dr. X. charges into the room as if it's a drug bust and the gig is up. He says something to you, but you have to ask him to repeat it, since you're already nervous, because there seems to have been a mix-up, and this guy might think you are an asshole who lacks courtesy when actually you have a ton of courtesy and are the kind of patient who likes to bake cookies for your doctor and hear about their kids.

So Dr. X. sits in his chair, pulls up to his state-of-the-art computer, the new tool he was assured would simplify his life, and squints at the screen while he types and fires off questions.

Any burning while you pee?

Are we up to date on our immunizations?

Any pain in the abdomen?

I didn't like any of it. The sign, the speed, the computers that had begun inserting themselves squarely between patient and doctor. But let me tell you, when you love someone with a severe disability and complex medical problems, a person who falls through every crack in the sidewalk of society, a person not written in its margins but erased from the footnotes altogether, you know you can't afford to lose this doctor.

Not only that, but getting Wendy there to see him was like taking your piano in for a tuning. She weighed a mere hundred pounds, but somehow she had the strength of a high school wrestling team. And sometimes, in the midst of the production of getting her and her hundred-pound wheelchair into our own non-wheelchair-friendly van, she got mad. Her shows were on, damnit! Winter was bloody cold. And asking a person with no short-term memory and no impulse control to sit and wait nicely for the doctor is a great way to unleash the hounds.

She had a right to get mad. Life handed her good cards, then took them away. It was a raw deal. Sometimes people would spout garbage to us, like, her disability was "a blessing in disguise," or "God's plan." Please. *Please.* Her life was *hard*. It was relentlessly hard. And the person who had to shoulder the hardest part of it was her. In fact, what I would have labelled the bad times actually turned out to be good times in the narrative arc of her life, because, really, after the age of twenty-one, it kept getting worse.

Two really horrible things had happened as a result of her childhood brain surgery. The first was the post-operative men-ingitis that took everything away from her. Sight. Normal speech. Bladder control. Also proprioception—the ability to know where the body is in space and time. Short-term memory. Balance. Fine motor skills. Gross motor skills. The ability to reason. The chance to have children, something she dreamed and spoke of until very late in her life. All of it gone, gone, gone.

The second horrible thing was due to an inexplicable rewiring of the taste centres in her brain, and it was totally unexpected: she fell in love with country music.

This was *really* horrible for the rest of us because in addition to being partly blind, Wendy was also partly deaf. The radio in our house was cranked up as loud as it would go and tuned to CKLQ, the local country music channel, for up to eighteen hours a day. And while CKLQ was blaring, the television would be on PBS, set to *Grand Ole Opry* or *Austin City Limits.* All at the *same time.* And Wendy would be sitting in her pink bedroom—Wendy loved pink bedspreads and pink clothes and pink-clad china dolls and pink cakes and pink birthday candles—listening to this assault on the senses and bouncing away in a dance that mostly involved bending her knees over and over while she tried to avoid falling on her head. She would lean against her hospital TV table on wheels, the one where she sometimes insisted on eating all her meals, her face in *Opry* and an ear angled towards CKLQ, singing along to such classics as "There's a Tear in My Beer" in a voice that wavered like the pulsing of a washing machine. She had scanning speech, with a lilting rhythmic disturbance to it, because one of the parts of her brain that was damaged by surgery and meningitis was the cerebellum, the so-called "little brain." Sounds cute, adorable. But the cerebellum is really a sophisticated integration centre. All sensory info from the brain and spinal cord goes to the cerebellum, and it's in charge of figuring out where to move you in space—specifically, voluntary movements. The cerebellum is the Martha Graham of the central nervous system. It choreographs movements, normally making them elegant, seamless. Posture. Balance. Coordination. Intelligible speech. Sorry, Wendy, can't have those anymore! Can't get toothpaste onto a brush! Can't get that toothbrush into your mouth! Might be able to poke your eye out with it, though, or slather toothpaste on your cornea. And that speech, that scanning, tremulous, slow-pitch voice: you're stuck with it for the rest of your life. The content will be normal. It will be perfect, actually—pristine, grammatically flawless, and your observations will be fascinating and idiosyncratic. But nobody will know that about you, because the minute you open your mouth, quaking in that wheelchair because the cerebellum also supervises the torso, your trunk and hands flying, liquid spilling everywhere if you even try to manage so much as a glass of water—

people will look at you and think . . . well, you know what they'll think. I know what they thought, because of the damaging things people were willing to say outright. Please have the *courtesy* not to bring your retarded child to our school for regular people. Please have the *courtesy* not to use this rehabilitation swimming pool, because it's only for people who can be rehabilitated. Please have the *courtesy* to teach your handicapped daughter some manners. She's rude. She swears. She learned a few choice words post-tumour, let me tell you, but she had every right to those. I have a difficult time getting through a day in the hospital without a supply of assorted cusswords (please have the *courtesy* not to swear when you learn there is not one empty bed anywhere in the entire hospital and the emergency department is full).

My sister suffered near total exclusion from society. I watched her face that exile.

Country music. Kenny Rogers, for instance. Back then, whether he was the guest on *Grand Ole Opry* or just taking a turn torturing me via CKLQ, I never listened closely to the likes of him. So it was by fluke one day that I saw one of his albums, *The Gambler*, in the window of an old record store. This was right around the time my associate dean's role had started to go sour. I didn't know why I was doing it anymore. I was miserable and wallowing, already thinking about quitting. Seeing that record cover brought tears to my eyes. Suddenly, as if my brain were tuned in to the station, I could almost hear his gravelly voice: *sometimes you just have to walk away.*

I stood on the sidewalk practically crying. It was silly to be choking up at the memory of a country song, but it felt like a sign I'd been looking for. Later that night, noodling around on my phone, I looked up the rest of the lyrics. I'd listened to it a thousand times in my childhood, belted out by my sister in a key discernable only to her, but somehow I'd never really heard the words. What I had to know. What I had to do. And even the best thing Wendy could hope for. There it was, laid out for me in the plainest terms. *You just hope you die in your sleep.*

Was the Gambler a pessimist? Was he a prophet? Or was he just burnt out?

o   o   o

I KNOW NOW that the doctor with the "courtesy" notice in his office was probably suffering from burnout. Burnout in physicians is a public health crisis. The term was first defined by a man named Herbert Freudenberger, but the defining scholarly work on burnout is the legacy of another psychologist, Dr. Christina Maslach. Burnout is an ugly trifecta: depersonalization, the feeling that one's work doesn't matter, and a low sense of personal accomplishment. An "erosion of the soul." Maslach gave us this language, and her scale—the Maslach Burnout Inventory—has been used in the biggest studies on burnout in health care.

But Christina Maslach did something much more amazing than define a syndrome. In 1971, a psychologist named Philip Zimbardo decided to use volunteers to replicate the conditions of prison, hoping to illustrate the latent capacity of individuals to fall into stereotypical roles. In what later became known as the famous Stanford Prison Experiment, Zimbardo and his colleagues recruited young, healthy men to play the parts of both prisoners and guards. They created a simulated prison facility, incarcerating half the participants and putting the other half in charge of the prison. What followed over the next several days was mayhem. "Guards" became depersonalized and callous, especially once they were hidden behind opaque reflective sunglasses, the kind that made it impossible for anyone to see their eyes. The inmates, referred to only by their numbers, became both defiant and passive, seeming to detach from their personal identities. Everything escalated; soon no behaviour was deemed unacceptable and the whole thing descended into chaos. Insulated from the rest of the world within an extreme hierarchy, the volunteers created their own playbook.

How does Christina Maslach fit into this? She went to the "prison" as a consultant on day five or six. She was the fiftieth person who attended the scene, and unlike the forty-nine before her, she was astounded. She reportedly shouted, "It's terrible what you are doing to these boys!" She shamed her colleague, Zimbardo, into stopping the experiment; although—a footnote—she later married him. But the fact is, Zimbardo stopped the experiment because of her, because she sounded the alarm. She saw—and named—the gorilla in the room.*

So what does it mean that she also helped interpret the phenomenon of the doctor of my childhood, staring at his computer screen, sitting under a rude sign that stressed out patients like me? He had his quirks, but he was hardly a monster. Whenever Wendy fell and sliced something open, he'd always come and stitch her up himself, a job his colleagues in the ER were only too happy to relinquish, my parents glad for his familiar face and skilled hands. Sometimes, on days when he seemed less stressed, Wendy would call him an old goat or peer at him through her Coke-bottle

---

* In recent years, some descriptions of the experiment and its conclusions have come under fire, but nobody questions that Dr. Maslach was the one who put a stop to the stupidity.

glasses and mumble under her breath that he was gorgeous, and he'd share a chuckle with my parents, then deride the government for failing to provide her with services.

That doctor had entered another experiment as a normal person with good intentions. The experiment was called medical school, and something had happened to him in the process. Sometimes, even if he behaved like a guard, I suspect he also felt like a prisoner.

I have not forgiven the sign, but I understand that doctor better now. He was a casualty of the experiment. His distress was directed outward. Mine was directed inward. That is the biggest difference between us.

Who Will Go with Me?

t's the afternoon session now, in the great hall. We start by sitting for fifteen minutes, cushions spread out, chairs in a semicircle. This is very church group-y for my tastes. I find a cushion, assume the pretzel. I notice a shift in my mood, a black mist that seems to move in and out of me when I breathe. Noticing what arises. Impatience. How many more days of this? It's a bit nice, but tiring, like spending way too long in a hot tub. Images of oatmeal and the egg pyramid and a cold room right out of the convent. I wonder if I can get an extra blanket without a ration stamp. I notice my mind is wandering. I don't usually notice. Is this progress?

Ron rings his stupid bell.

He says he is checking in. How is everybody doing?

Lots of people say they're fabulous. The woman who talks way too much says Mick and Ron are hitting the nail on the head, meeting every one of her needs.

Except for a psychiatrist.

Yes, I added that.

Ron puts up a slide with one word on it: suffering. Then he flips to van Gogh's painting, *Old Man in Sorrow.*

He asks: What does everyone notice?

I notice he's hunched over. He's either super-depressed or hanging out on a commode until a nurse comes to help him back to bed.

Blue. People are noticing lots of blue, naming the shades. Cornflower and marine, all those second-rate crayons you only move to after the real blue is used up.

I don't know much about art, but I know this is a self-portrait, and van Gogh looks rough in this picture. He's painted himself in the universal posture of despair.

I've sat like that, with my head propped in my hands, usually because I think I might have killed somebody.

Ron asks how people feel looking at it. The group spits out a bunch of predictable adjectives.

I'm remembering the first time medicine put me in this pose. Sitting in the locker room, post-call, head in my hands, just like van Gogh. Shaking so bad I couldn't get the combination on my lock. Saying into my wet palms, *I can't do this. I can't do this anymore. The stakes are just too high.*

I'd been on call in the hospital every second day for no less than six days. Call regulations said you weren't allowed to do more than one-in-four, but that limit was just an average over the month. If someone on the rotation was on vacation, or sick, you could end up doing one-in-three. Or in this case, a stretch of one-in-two. You might be part of a skeleton crew of four interns and residents doing call solo, or, when you were on internal medicine, taking call together as a team but covering the entire medicine service, not setting foot out of the hospital, often looking after more than a hundred patients combined. At work and awake for 96 of those 144 hours. Would you want that person even walking your dog? Without a note of irony, we call that being on call in-house. Just not in your *own* house. That's why they referred to us as "the residents," because we lived in the damn place. We might as well have gotten our mail there. Sometimes you wondered whether there was even a point in going home post-call—around noon if you were lucky, statistically more likely to get into a vehicle accident on your way there—only to come back the next morning at 7 or 8 a.m. for a "regular" ten-hour day, until that next on-call shift.

In the hospital, you had a call room, with a bed and a lamp and a desk, but you had no expectation of sleeping—maybe, at best, getting to lie down for an hour or two somewhere between 4 and 6 a.m. *Maybe.* On an *amazing* day. You ate meals when you could, usually several hours late, sometimes ordering food with the other residents, sometimes going hungry, because it seemed like so much work to hunt and gather anything more than a Diet Coke and a bag of stale chips from the vending machine. Your pager going off constantly. Patients crashing, needing admission, EKGs and arterial blood gases and acute medical situations: all of that your problem. Everything in that massive hospital felt like your problem, and even though it was full of other interns and residents and somewhere off in a far corner some staff surgeons and anesthetists and possibly a fifth-year resident covering in the ICU, sometimes you could go for hours without seeing any-one other than the patients and the nurses, all of whom wanted to believe that *you*—with your degree in biochemistry, or maybe even English, and an average of four years of medical school and now a few months of internship under your belt—were somehow capable of solving their complicated medical problems *and* of operating without the sleep that even the hospital union recognized was crucial to the janitor's ability to properly disinfect the ward. And he, unlike you, was entitled to breaks.

That shift, the one when I wept by the lockers, I'd been called in the late evening to see a young woman I'd met for the first time that night, a woman with a new diagnosis of heart failure. She had just moved to Toronto; she was from somewhere on the East Coast. She had no family, no friends, no one at the bedside. She was confused, and I was too. Why had she suddenly become unreasonable, hissing at the nurses, tossing things, overturning the bedpans? What could be causing her delirium? Nothing was obviously wrong. Her vitals were stable, her chest X-ray unchanged. I examined her, couldn't find anything amiss. What would I tell the staff doctor if I called him at home, beyond the fact that a patient had just thrown a cup of ice chips in my general direction? I couldn't name the unsettled feeling in my gut, a feeling I'd never had before. Or maybe I confused it with the sensory hell of profound sleep deprivation, the pins and needles in limbs too tired to be moved, the leaden heaviness of every breath. I wasn't experienced enough to know that the moments when we don't know what's going on are the moments we need to treat with fear and reverence, because we can't predict what's going to happen next.

I stumbled back to the call room and collapsed on the bed, shivering under the hospital flannel before falling quickly into a thick, dark void of sleep. Less than an hour later: another page. I woke up, unsure of where I was, unable to even remember what service I was covering. I called the ward; it was the nurse who had paged me earlier about the young woman. *That lady isn't responding.* Suddenly wide awake, heart pounding, running to her room in a state of terror. Pushing past the nurse, finding the woman barely breathing, shouting that she wasn't responding because she was *unconscious*, yelling at them to call a code blue, thus summoning a crash cart and the intensive care team. My stomach felt like it was falling out of my body, descending into the heart of the world. The code team arriving in a stampede, filling the room with chaos. *No pulse. No pulse. No pulse.* The team intubating and ventilating her, and still no pulse. Nothing was bringing it back. Me saying more than once, pleading with the universe, repeating it like an incantation, *Please let her be all right.* The code lasted an hour. The fifth-year ICU resident ended it. The woman was officially, irrevocably, irreversibly dead: a shocking, sudden death. I couldn't stop shaking. I told the senior resident: *I don't know if I missed something. Did I miss something?* Leaning against the wall, teeth chattering like a wind-up toy. Asking him over and over, repeating myself: *What did I miss? What would you have done? What should I have done differently? Should I have done something differently? Is there anything I could have done differently?* He wasn't unkind, but he was cool, clinical. He didn't chastise or comfort me. He just told me, matter-of-factly: "That's why we call it a teaching hospital, Jill. This is how you learn."

How you learn what, exactly? I only learned one thing that day: It was my fault. That's what I thought: *It was all my fault.* As if I had intentionally cut into this woman's already damaged heart with a knife. A sick heart, as thin and fragile as a cellophane bag. Long before the night she died, her life was on a trajectory I could probably only have nudged, not changed. But I didn't know that then. I had no one to compare her to. And so I left the hospital that morning believing, really believing that a woman was dead because of me.

I've carried that case ever since. I've talked about it with a few residents, usually after they've experienced some similar trauma or perceived failure and I'm ushering them into this exclusive club, where membership is for life.

I don't want to look at van Gogh, the old man in despair. He should keep that to himself. I stand up, tiptoe through a maze of cushions, quietly exit the hall.

The mirrorless washroom feels like a refuge, as if I can't follow myself in there. I splash some water on my face, lean against the white wall and peer out the screened window. I pull out my phone. Yes, Ron, I know you suggested we put them away for the time we're here, but seriously, if I don't answer messages for five days, people will assume I'm dead.

I text Eric: *Are the boys ok?*

Of course the boys are okay. What's he going to say—that he hasn't seen one of them since Tuesday? The boys are resilient, and well attached, and my husband is an amazing dad, not just a watered-down substitute for me.

I google *Old Man in Sorrow*. There he is, on my phone, with few paragraphs of random information, including a subtitle in brackets: *At Eternity's Gate.*

Just before he killed himself, van Gogh painted this self-portrait after getting out of the psychiatric hospital.

I hadn't known that—that he killed himself. Apparently, my knowledge of art history is worse than my ability to spot a gorilla on an X-ray.

He went to be near his physician, Dr. Gachet, whom he sometimes painted.

I google Dr. Gachet. A picture appears on my screen, a deep blue rendering of another very sad man. This blue, blue doctor is gazing at Vincent as he paints, with a look on his face that is probably identical to the look I'd see in a mirror right now, if there were a mirror on the wall in this weird washroom at the Doctor Rehab in the Woods. I enlarge the picture on my phone.

Dr. Gachet is not taking new patients. Please have the courtesy not to ask.

What's that look?

It's Dr. Gachet, sitting with it all in that moment, whatever is being given to him. Containment. Holding all the things he can diagnose but not change. It hurts to do that, if you're doing it well. If it's difficult for him, we don't necessarily want to know.

I go back into the hall. People are working in small groups again, talking quietly. Jodie is hanging out by the door, nursing a cup of coffee. She's foraged one for me too.

She hands it to me. "Where were you, smoking?"

"I can't even find anywhere to buy drugs around here."

"I'm waiting for you."

"That's why I came back."

Jodie points at a pair of cushions in the corner. We sit down.

"You joke about everything," she says.

"Except coffee, remember?"

"I remembered. Do you want to talk first?"

"About what?"

"A time when we were present with suffering."

Suddenly I'm tired. The sky outside is crisp, cloudless. I can smell damp earth through the open window. I'd like to be out on the grass by the water, upstream, by the little mill.

"Do your patients see you, Jodie?"

117

She looks at me, raises an eyebrow.

"When you're in the room with them, talking to them. Do you think they see you?"

She adjusts the cushion, spills some coffee on the hardwood floor, wipes it up with her sock.

"What do you want them to see?"

I pull out my phone. I show her the picture of Dr. Gachet.

"You want them to see this guy?" She studies my phone. "Who painted this?"

"Van Gogh. It's his doctor."

"Give me that. Devices are contraband. We're supposed to be talking about suffering."

"This guy looks like he's suffering. And how is this not a conversation about suffering?

"Feeling unknown might be the worst social pain there is."

"Besides working with blue-haired Canadians?"

"That's in a class of its own."

"So what's a time you were fully present with suffering?"

"Not including breakfast with you this morning?"

"Cut it out, Horton."

I settle on my cushion. I find a bit of oatmeal on one of my sleeves. I take a deep breath.

A Time I Was Present with Suffering
A tragic story wherein the hero dies and the heroine is emotionally maimed

By Jill H.

Stan was about forty years old. I met him when I was a third-year resident on the neurology service. He was a karate instructor.

He looked like an ad for your favourite gym or maybe even an illegal supplement that was too good to be true. That's how fit and healthy he was. He had a five-year-old son.

It started with his legs. He noticed they were numb, or weak, or both. He saw a few GPs, and they told him he'd pulled something. Or he had a slipped disc. But things kept getting worse, and one day he couldn't pass urine. So he went to the ER, and the doctor there sent him for a CT scan of his back. And they saw something in his spinal cord that the doctor told him looked like a "shadow," and the doctor made references to *The Karate Kid*, which by then was an old movie, and this was cheesy and cliché and left him with no meaningful information about what was actually happening in his spine.

But of course, everybody thought this was cancer.

Stan was super smart. He was really positive. This was a guy who had read more philosophy than me, but also mushier stuff, like *Jonathan Livingston Seagull* and *The Alchemist*. He liked me to be upbeat too. He got that something really bad was evolving, but karate had taught him to believe in the power of mind over body. So every time I came in to tell him something terrible, like, *your calcium level is high*, which in a situation like this is pretty much cancer leaving a "sorry I missed you" card, Stan took it like it was a training exercise.

He needed a biopsy of the "shadow." We arranged it, but it kept getting cancelled. Every day he got bumped for a trauma that had to go to the OR, or some more urgent problem than a shadow in your spine. And every day when I got the news that he'd been bumped, even though each day he'd been fasting since midnight, I had to go in to his room, look him in the eye and tell him once again there wouldn't be a biopsy, apologizing for something I had no control over but that still made me feel horrible. He never

119

once blamed me. He could see I was helpless. He was helpless too. By this point he had no ability to move his lower extremities. And yet, every day, he still managed to ask me how I was doing.

"Oh, I'm fine," I'd always tell him. "It's you I'm worried about."

Then this SARS thing happened. Right in the middle of this. The hospitals in Toronto went on lockdown. Because of a suspected exposure, even though it was incredibly low risk, I got stuck in a quarantine in my apartment, which frankly was the best thing to happen to me during my entire residency. I slept and read trashy magazines, and Eric got me delicious takeout. I stayed out of the hospital for five glorious days. When I went back, Stan had finally had his biopsy. They'd transferred him onto the neurosurgery service. Now I didn't have to go see him every day, because he was under their care. And to be honest, in a way I was glad I didn't have to see him. There was such a mismatch between his bravery and the grim conclusion we were inching towards, I almost couldn't handle it.

A few weeks passed. Visitors of patients who weren't imminently dying were banned from hospitals in the Greater Toronto Area, while officials tried to figure out how SARS was spreading. I thought of Stan, alone in his room, his wife and child unable to be near him. But of course, I wasn't banned because I was hospital staff. So one day, after I'd finished rounding on the neurology patients, I resolved to go see him. I took a book I'd bought for him, some dumb thing called *Life Is Mind Over Matter*, which really seemed hilarious to me at that point, because after three years of residency beating me to a pulp, my own mind was pretty much of the opinion that nothing mattered anymore.

I went to the neurosurgery ward. I knocked on his door and

pushed it open hesitantly, afraid of what I might see. We all had to wear yellow gowns and plastic face shields because of SARS, and I must have looked like Big Bird walking into that room. He smiled when he saw me, a smile I didn't think I deserved. I sat down next to him. I asked how he was doing. He said he was doing okay. He was waiting for the final biopsy results. I'd read in the chart that they'd given him a preliminary result: a really bad kind of poorly differentiated lymphoma. This basically meant he was going to die, but not until we had poisoned him with chemotherapy that probably wouldn't do a thing for him anyway. Did he know that? I wasn't sure if he knew that. Should I tell him? It wasn't really my place, and I didn't know how much he wanted to know just yet. Sometimes we say we want to know "everything" but might not pick "everything" if we actually knew what was behind that door. The curse of knowledge.

I pulled *Life Is Mind Over Matter* out of my bag. I stupidly said maybe it would help. It was the dumbest gift of all time, a parka in the desert for a man who wouldn't live to see any other season. But he turned it over in his hands a few times and said thank you at least five times. He was so grateful for this useless book that I started to feel sick about giving it to him. Then he asked how I was doing, especially with all this SARS stuff going on. I told him I was fine, which was a lie, because all of us were terrified we were going to get SARS and die foaming at the mouth and choking on our own secretions. I was panicking every morning walking into the hospital, picturing my parents getting a phone call that I was in the ICU on life support with an incurable mystery illness. This wasn't hyperbole. An internist at one of the other hospitals got it and almost died. But I didn't dump that on Stan. I told him we'd get through it and that with time things would settle down. I told him I believed that hope mattered, and in his case nothing was settled until they knew the final results of that biopsy for sure. I told him my sister had cancer when she was six, and everyone expected her to die, and here we were thirty years later and she was still alive. He said, Wow! But of course, I didn't show him her picture, because I didn't want Stan to realize that it was possible to come out on the other side of cancer treatment looking like the Bride of Frankenstein when you went in a handsome stunt-double karate instructor or a perfect little girl.

And the truth was, I *knew* he wasn't coming out on the other side. I knew he was a condemned man. I looked at him clutching that stupid book and suddenly I couldn't hold it back anymore. I burst into tears. I remember telling him over and over again how sorry I was. I remember that at some point I wasn't wearing my Big Bird mask anymore, because I knew I wasn't going to get SARS from Stan. The only thing Stan was going to give me was a broken heart. We were just holding each other and wailing. And I remember that it felt like Stan was comforting me, because he just kept saying it was okay, and when I'd say I was fine, I was just so sorry, he'd say I know, touching my face and telling me he would be okay, saying it's okay, but of course it wasn't okay, so that only made me cry more.

That yellow, yellow gown, a canary, a coal mine. And the photo on the bedside table of his son, Aidan. Aidan was missing a tooth and smiling, and one of the reasons I cried so hard was that I knew Aidan would soon be missing a dad.

Jodie is shaking her head. "That is so fucking sad." Jodie motions towards the prompts on the screen. "So what let you be present with his suffering?"

I think about her question.

"I didn't want to abandon him."

"More about that."

"I wouldn't want to be abandoned."

"Keep going. I feel like it matters."

"Could you stop channelling Dr. Phil?"

"Too late for that. What let you be there for him?"

"I wanted to go with him."

"What does that mean?"

"We all want someone who will go with us."

"Where?"

I pause. God, Stan would have loved this place. The ritual, the formalities. Ron's little Tibetan bell. Sensei Stan.

"My dad told me a story once. He really likes *Reader's Digest*. We used to have them all over the house. And for years I was in this terrible relationship."

"With *Reader's Digest*?"

"Fuck off, Jodie."

"I thought that's what you meant!"

"I was in a doomed relationship with a *guy*. Like, we made *no* sense. I'm trying to decide whether I stay with this person, okay? And I'm torn to pieces, and one day my dad is trying to be helpful and tells me, 'You know, I read in *Reader's Digest* that you need to ask yourself two questions in any relationship. *Where do I want to go?* and *Who will go with me?*"

"Those are good questions."

"I didn't think so. I told my dad he was old, he didn't really know anything about my life, and I didn't think I was going to find the answer to my problems in his stupid grade-eight level *Reader's Digest*. And so I keep dating this guy, right? Things get worse between us, and I mean, like, toxic waste-dump ugly. It's right before I start residency, and one day I pack up all my stuff and put it in storage, and I fly home for the week just to find the energy to break up with him, and then I go to my parents' house and I cry."

"And the house is still full of all those copies of *Reader's Digest*."

"Sure, Jodie. So I'm a mess, I'm in my pyjamas all week crying on the sofa, and one day my dad is trying to be helpful and he says, 'You know, I read once in *Reader's Digest* there are two questions you should ask in a relationship.'"

"And you're like, 'Dad, fuck off with the *Reader's Digest*.'"

"Totally! I said to him, 'You already told me that complete bullshit story about where do I want to go and who do I want to go with me.'

"And *he* said, 'You got the second question wrong.'"

Jodie purses her lips. "But you didn't."

"No, Jodie, I *did*. The second question isn't *Who do I want to go with me?* It's *Who will go with me?* Get it? It isn't just who you *want* to go with you. It's who *will* go."

She thinks about it for a few seconds, then nods approvingly. "Your dad sounds wise."

"He's pretty smart."

"So you were willing to go with Stan. Into his suffering."

I nod. The memory of him fills the room. That wonderful, wonderful man. Frozen in space and time, his life cut off in mid-kick.

"Why, Jill?" Jodie asks. "Put your finger on why."

"That's why I'm *here*."

"You mean at the retreat?"

"I mean in *life*. That's what I'm here to do. I don't know how else to explain it."

"Sounds like you need more *Reader's Digest*." Jodie frowns. "Hold on a sec." She gropes for something in her pocket. It's a phone. It's *my* phone, the one she confiscated. She takes it out, looks at the screen disapprovingly.

"Who's Eric?"

"My husband. What did he say?"

She does her best classic horror flick voice. "The baby dove is *alive*."

For now, I think to myself.

15

A Life Sentence

We get a break in the late afternoon. I put on my coat and running shoes, and head out to the grounds and the stream. It's cold here for April. There's a dampness that permeates everything, a chill I can't shake no matter how much wool I'm wrapped in. We're not supposed to have any food in our rooms, but I found an old granola bar in the outer pouch of my suitcase. It's my only contraband. I cross the long driveway, walk to the half-circle bridge that spans the creek.

My phone is back in my pocket. I sneak it out and glance at it, nestling it in my palm. Fifteen new emails. Something from my secretary. Something about a school concert I'm going to miss anyway. A collection of headlines from the *New England Journal of Medicine*. I skim it. Stuff I already know. Stuff I don't need to know. Stuff I think I might be supposed to know. Stuff I have no hope of knowing. Something from a student. *Dr. Horton, I'm sorry to be bothering you as your auto-reply says you are away but I am really struggling to cope right now.* Hazel, do you read *anything*? How do you not know that I quit? I'm the one who's struggling to cope right now, and half of it is because of you weasels. Not that you personally are a weasel. I ran into Hazel once in the grocery store with her mom and, aside from looking so uncomfortable I thought she might turn inside out, she actually seemed really nice.

Just like that, I'm not here anymore. I'm back in my office with a waiting room full of panicked students, reliving those last lectures, the snickering in the back row. But even worse, I'm missing the water, missing the crispness of the cold, missing the red, red cardinal that just landed over in the grass. Missing all of it, because my mind has a dog's tendency to lick wounds repeatedly. An instinctive, evolutionary behaviour—one that might have been helpful in the wild. But some dogs lick their wounds again, and again, until their flesh is stripped down to the bone by all that licking, and still the dog won't stop. Yet another behaviour that no longer serves a purpose, creates a host of other problems.

I put away my phone and open the granola bar. It has a waxy sheen to it, the gleam of elderly food that shouldn't be eaten. I throw it into Siddhartha's stream. I wait for the water to reveal everything in my life and everything I have done in my life. But of course, it doesn't. The granola bar disappears beneath the uneven surface of the water, colliding with a floating stick before it's gone for good.

Leaning over the railing, I notice someone has tucked a note into the crack in the wood. I feel an irrational rush of excitement, like I've found an oracle. I pull it out, unfold the damp paper, and read:

The stream of consciousness.

It's funny; it should make me laugh. But I'm affronted that someone like me has already been here and stolen my line.

Did they also give up sherry with tutors, cackling with friends in front of a fire at Oxford? What if I'd taken that path instead, and hadn't gone to medical school?

That little knot again, the lump in my throat from the Zendo. That spot, that hurt, that place with no map.

I start walking. Mud gums up my boots, the ground sucking me into wet earth. In the distance, by a small clearing overlooking a brown pool, there's a bench and a statue of the Buddha. I can feel the smell of earth in my teeth and jaw. I reach the little clearing. I put out my hand to touch the back of the Buddha's head, keeping my fingers on smooth stone while I circle around to see his face.

But he has no face. What I thought was a sitting form is just a shape, a wide sphere with another sphere set carefully on top. For some reason this feels like a circus trick. I rap the back of the faceless Buddha head with my knuckles, which really hurts my hand. Okay, I just punched a rock for not looking like Buddha. Is that why I'm here?

What if I could let go of expectations?

The day's sessions have steered me towards a little babbling brook of my own. I can hear what the stream is saying. It's saying *I* was faceless when I was a resident. That nobody really knew me. That I abandoned myself, that I let myself be sacrificed to something I thought was greater than me. That the sacrifice I thought I was making for patients was actually for a sick and pointless system, the necessity of particular types of hardship only an illusion. It had to be difficult; medicine will always be so. But did it have to be so difficult it made me sick? That's the betrayal I'm grappling with right now, a feeling I don't have to explain to one other person at this retreat. Imagine being told to swim across a treacherous river to rescue someone on the other side. You brave that river. You're bitten, you're maimed, you're shuddering and waterlogged, and you almost drown. When you haul yourself out on the banks, you reach out to touch that person, the one you did all of this for; you say, *I came. I'm here for you.* And then you see the trick: it isn't a person at all. It's a column of stone. This wasn't the emergency. The emergency is somewhere else, and you missed the whole thing, because you were busy swimming across the river. You could have taken a raft. There was a raft right there the whole time, on shore, but they made you swim to the rock pile, because that's what everybody does, and now you're supposed to tell the next ones, the ones coming up behind you, they have to do the same thing.

You might feel conflicted about all this. You might wonder how you were talked into doing something so dangerous. You might feel angry, and misled, and devastated. You might have to make up a story about why you did that to yourself. But you did it because, in the process of becoming a doctor, normal dissolves like white powder in warm liquid. It's not *normal* to go without sleep. It's not normal to watch people die, then go drink a cup of coffee and talk about your plans for the weekend. It's not normal to be blamed for not knowing what you couldn't possibly know, to have to carry that weight by yourself across the river. You set off on what you think is a Hero's Journey but turns out to be the Stanford Prison Experiment. Normal completely disappears from your life, melts away until it isn't even a memory. Christina Maslach doesn't come to stop it.

Every one of us here has asked ourselves over and over, *Am I the problem? Is the problem really just that I'm not cut out for this?* When she hissed that I should stop telling people I was applying to medical school, was that girl I knew in university really seeing the real me? Maybe I wasn't cut out for this. Maybe that's why I've suffered so much along the way.

There was another person who saw me, a boy in grade eight, and he was kind of nice and probably feels bad about this, because who would want to be judged for the rest of their life by the shittiest thing they ever did to somebody else when they were thirteen? He wrote a sentence in my yearbook that I might as well have tattooed on my heart—the truth nobody would tell me to my face, the reason everything in my life felt completely wrong. That boy's words came back to me like a Saturday morning television jingle when the Dutchman told me there was still a way I could be perfect. Cancelling out all the nice things my friends had scrawled about me, that boy wrote one sentence in big, messy letters, an epitaph for my junior high years:

You're pretty smart, just lose some weight.

There it still is. Moses on Sinai. A noble truth handed down to me in a grade eight yearbook. Things said in innocence, in the cruelty of youth, things we believe about ourselves our whole lives.

In the session this afternoon Ron said to keep a notebook handy, so when thoughts come to us we can scribble them down, write narratives, notice who comes to visit. I have a tiny Moleskine in my pocket. I settle down on the bench and write the words across the top in capital letters.

You're pretty smart. Just lose some weight.
You're pretty smart. Just lose some weight.
You're pretty smart. Just lose some weight.

Then I put a line through the whole page. I wait a minute, then write:

Dearest Ron and Mick,

I'm fumbling with some basic building blocks of life, some central incompetence that nobody has diagnosed. This isn't how do I read a chest CT or how do I appreciate van Gogh. This is being forty and wondering, how come I don't even know how to breathe?

Kindest regards,
Jill

I draw a line through that too. I think about the step I don't want to take. What was the word that elbowed me in the ribs in the Zendo? *Forgiveness.*

My pen hovers over the lined pages as if they are a Ouija board, and from somewhere in the recesses of my mind, a name appears.

The Terrible Story of Mr. Ripple

A chilling tale of lifelong emotional disfigurement

By JILL H.

Mr. Ripple was almost ninety. He came in to the hospital the colour of a bedsheet. We found several fist-sized masses on his liver and kidneys, his belly distended like the big end of a lightbulb, full of blood and cancer, both those organs failing. We met at three in the morning. We laughed over some silly things. I tried to comfort him. The only thing I had to do that with was words.

When I told him the results of his imaging, he said, "Thank you for telling me the truth." He asked if I could stay and talk to his wife. I'd been up for thirty hours, but I waited for her and told her what we'd found and sat and cried with her, my fellow standing in the corner the whole time, nodding in sympathy and agreement. He said I did a good job. I wiped tears out of my eyes and went home to bed.

The next day, the staff physician suggested we consult a surgeon, even though she said it would be futile. She said the wife and children might be the ones who needed the consultation, that it would be for closure. I said he had no children. But I did what she wanted me to do. I put in the consult.

The surgeon on call was a short, smug, greasy young staff doctor who always had a look on his face like the people around him smelled awful. The senior residents all said he was overly confident and had terrible judgment. He reviewed the case. He went into Mr. Ripple's room. He came out and announced to the team and to my attending physician, "These could be abscesses. If they are, they'll just melt away with antibiotics." They just melt away! Like cotton candy! And who wouldn't want cotton candy abscesses instead of the deadly cancer diagnosed by the stupid female first-year resident?

The surgeon left. I went back to see Mr. Ripple. The whole feeling in the room had changed. Mr. Ripple was sure I had unnecessarily told his wife he was going to die, and now she was even having chest pain. Mr. Ripple screamed that it was totally wrong, that I was a person of unbelievable character, that he was going to write the hospital a letter about me and it wouldn't be very nice, that he would never forgive me for what I had done.

How to describe the scar of those words, the brand they left on the softest parts of me, searing my tender skin?

Nothing could be less like cotton candy.

I went out to the nursing desk, shaking. I told my fellow what had happened. I thought he would come back into the room with me, tell Mr. Ripple he'd agreed with everything I'd said, get me out of the line of fire, explain it was his opinion I had offered, not my own. He was very kind, but he didn't like conflict. He didn't want to deal with the patient's anger, didn't want it branding him, because he could see it looked painful. He shrugged and gave a cryptic half-smile; he said to me, for the second time that year, "This is how you learn." He walked off the unit, whistling.

What am I supposed to be learning? I was screaming inside.

But here was the worst part: I still had to face Mr. Ripple each morning and sponge up his hatred of me, like the worthless, helpless dog I was. I was almost sick to my stomach going into that room. My senior, the second-year internal medicine resident who dealt with the logistics of how the team ran every day, wouldn't assign somebody else to his care. He said continuity was critical. He didn't know continuity was me getting crushed like a bug every time I had to walk into that room.

From the moment the greasy surgeon had become involved, Mr. Ripple spoke to me like I was an insufferable handmaid. He shouted at me to tell him what antibiotics the surgeon had recommended and acted as if he'd caught me red-handed when, after a morning of running myself ragged post-call, I still had not been able to sort out the correct dosing with the pharmacist. In less than seventy-two hours, I had become *persona non grata*. I had cared about him; I had cried with him. And now Mr. Ripple was treating me like I was the person who had given him the disease that was going to end his life.

I understand that patients and families have negative transference. I had it towards all the doctors who failed Wendy, doctors I never even met. I was angry at all of them, but it wasn't just because I thought they made mistakes. It was because everybody had acted like it was *no big deal* that they'd made those mistakes. That's what got me upset. But even then, I wasn't sure I could imagine making those doctors scapegoats for every one of my grievances with the universe. Surely Mr. Ripple had to have known that if my staff physician had disagreed, she would never have allowed me to tell him he was going to die. Yet he and his wife continued to treat my staff doctor courteously, speaking to her about me with eye-rolls and stone faces; and for reasons I still don't understand, everyone let me take the fall.

I guess I was a safer receptacle for their hatred.

Mr. Ripple, whose ghostly pallor was perhaps another sign of the suffering that lay ahead for both of us, spent the last days of his life angry about my perceived incompetence. His wife did too.

Despite the antibiotics, he was dead exactly one week after we met. As everyone other than the surgeon had suspected, he did not have cotton candy abscesses.

o o o

135

"DON'T TELL ME we have homework?"

I hadn't heard anyone coming up behind me, but there's a man, another doctor, to my left. He's hovering by the faceless rock pile, watching me write.

I'm startled. I can't hide my unease. He sees this immediately, keeps a distance from the bench.

"Sorry for intruding."

I study him for a few seconds. Tall, lanky. Hair in a horseshoe pattern, a little garden border of fuzz around his mostly bare head. Physique like a bat. A purple Patagonia jacket. Gloves. Whenever I see a man in the woods wearing gloves, it crosses my mind he's a serial killer, but this guy looks like he'd injure himself twisting a cap off a bottle. Harmless.

"You can sit if you want."

He hesitates. I like him because he hesitated. I pat the bench with my hand, closing my notebook. He comes and sits next to me, offers me a gloved hand.

"I'm Roy."

"Jill. Where are you from?"

"Boston. You?"

"Canada."

"Too nonspecific."

This makes me chuckle. "Only a doctor would say that. Once I heard a man checking in at a hotel front desk. The clerk asked him how his drive was. He said, 'Uneventful.'"

"Anesthetist."

"Right?"

"Or a surgeon."

"But definitely a doctor."

"What are you?"

"Radiologist. You?"

"Internist."

"Condolences."

"You're not kidding."

Roy rubs his face with the back of his palm. I try to calculate his age. A mallard duck with an emerald green head lands in front of us. It shimmers, even in the dull light.

"Show-off." Roy flicks his hand at the duck. It waddles up the bank towards us, quacks at us a couple of times.

I call out to the duck. "Only doctors here right now, please."

"What were you writing?"

"Just something about a patient."

"What patient? You don't have to answer."

"Somebody who blamed me for something that wasn't my fault."

Roy nods. We both sit, contemplating the duck.

He taps his temple. "I have a file like that up here."

"I hear that."

"Do you meditate?"

"Not much. You?"

"I have been."

"Since when?"

Roy lets the question linger in the air for a while. He pulls a tissue out of his pocket, wipes his nose. "Since my wife left me for somebody else."

"Oh, I'm sorry." I *am* sorry, because he looks sad, like Mr. Rogers about to cry, and who wants to see that?

"Why are you here?" Roy looks at me with hound-dog eyes, glasses streaked with something oily.

"Not sure yet."

"Are you married?"

"Yes."

"Do you have kids?"

"Three."

"How old?"

"All under ten."

"Guessing you don't sleep much."

"Just between the pages."

"That's very literary."

"Well, I'm a failed writer."

"Interesting," he says, and he does sound interested. "Who confirmed you failed?"

"I got a letter."

"Did it bar you from writing again?"

"Yeah, in a handful of states."

"It's just a very heavy thing to say, 'I'm a failed' whatever-it-is. Maybe you're just a writer who hasn't published yet?"

"I guess that might be true."

"It's like a verdict, though, right? The way you said it? It's harsh. Like you're writing in a medical record."

"I *hate* the medical record." I wave my hand emphatically, and my pen falls in the mud.

Roy leans forward and picks it up, handing it back to me after he wipes it on his pants. Chivalry. I notice his pants are really ugly, some kind of corduroy that looks like mouldy fibreglass. God, this man needs sartorial help.

"Of course, you hate it as a writer as well as a doctor. Do you identify more as one or the other?"

I turn towards him a little. It's a lot of work, meeting all these doctors in the woods. He's leaning in. I feel him setting down his attention, almost plaintively, like an offering. Something in me softens.

"I haven't thought about it like that for a while."

"Why is that?"

"I guess I had to assimilate."

"What?"

"I had to become like everybody else."

He rolls his eyes. "I know what it means."

I pause because the male mallard is quacking at a female mallard off in the reeds. I call out to the duck: "Some kind of trouble in paradise?"

Roy persists. "You think *you* became like everybody else in medicine."

"Yes."

He's looking at me skeptically now. Roy, stop looking at me. You're acting like a big weirdo, and all I have with me to defend myself is a muddy pen, a Moleskine notebook and an expired inhaler I just discovered in my left pocket.

"Lady," he says, "this is so dubious."

"Sorry?"

"You have blue hair, and you're sitting in the woods talking to a duck." He laughs out loud. "You're the weirdest person here, and that's saying something."

What exactly is this guy's problem? He's an old coot in what looks like an athletic gingerbread-man onesie with fibreglass pants, and *he* just called *me* a weirdo?

He studies me through his smudged glasses. "You know who else is weird?"

"Um, *you're* pretty weird."

He flicks his fingers against the side of my knee and makes a *tsk* sound.

"Everybody who ever did anything interesting was weird. Name one writer you admire. Or one musician."

"Alice Munro."

"Who's that?"

I gasp. "What do you mean, who's that?"

Now Roy is really laughing. He's doubled over, trying to answer. His face is barnyard red. A perfect slice of the colour wheel.

"You should have seen your face."

"You should see *your* face. You look like a . . . goji berry or something."

"A . . . goji berry!'"

Roy is laughing so hard I might need to give him my inhaler. I don't find any of this as funny as he does.

"Tell me your favourite story by Alice," he says once he manages to stop laughing. "I'll download it and read it while we're here."

God, that is so annoying. *Alice.* Hemingway is Hemingway. Ondaatje is Ondaatje. Why is Munro *Alice*?

"Please?" he says. His laughter has passed. He's silent now, sitting on the bench, plaintive-looking. His skin is slack at the neck. He's back to just looking sad.

"Read 'Differently.'"

He mouths the word to himself so he won't forget. "What's it about?"

"It's about how we'd act if we believed we were going to die."

"What's the answer?"

I'm disproportionately annoyed with him, can't keep it from creeping into my voice. "She doesn't answer it, Roy. She knows you can't answer it, that's the point."

"Well, I'll read it." His voice is eager to please. "And all because a fantastically weird blue-haired woman recommended it to me."

The duck has tentatively waddled over to the reeds in the mud a few feet away from us. His head is shaped like a hammer.

"I like you," Roy says, sounding almost shy. "It's much easier to attach to other doctors. Have you noticed?"

There's something undeniably poignant about him. I'm picturing him going home to a rented apartment, eating takeout straight out of the fridge. Furniture from IKEA he hasn't bothered to assemble. No idea how frequently he should change bedsheets. I have a sudden, graphic sense of his loneliness. Sleeping in his underwear, the curtains letting in fillets of moonlight, making it difficult to sleep.

"Isn't that why veterans only want to be around other veterans?"

He nods. "Somebody once told me that residency was like an abusive relationship. They said if you're lucky, you survive."

"Yeah, we're lucky, all right."

"We are lucky." Roy pauses. The duck has wandered over into a triangle of weeds. "We're totally lucked up."

I don't mind this bat-shaped man, even if he did basically call me crazy. I'm never going to see him again after this week. I can say whatever I want.

Roy is squinting up at the tree line. "There's a falcon up there."

"I can't see it."

"A symbol of war. You must know that as a writer."

"Bad time to be a mouse."

"Hunt or be hunted."

I turn towards him. "Since you like symbols so much, there's this 'game' called Blue Whale. Have you heard of it?"

"Like a board game?"

"It's supposedly a deranged Internet scheme, though it might just be an urban legend. Where an asshole preys on some vulnerable person and grooms them to commit suicide through a series of desensitizing acts."

Roy sits up straight. "Well, that's fucking evil."

"Do you think it's a metaphor for what happens to us? Like, we hand over our control and it gives people licence to abuse us. And we're surrounded by suffering and death, and after a certain point we're willing to keep doing the crazy things they're telling us to do, and it stops seeming like a huge deal to die." I pause again, watching his face to see if he thinks *I'm* crazy. "And maybe it even stops seeming like a big deal to kill yourself."

"Medicine *as* the Blue Whale."

"Yes."

"And it's why so many doctors are killing themselves. Or thinking about it." He pauses. "But isn't that because of burnout?"

"God, no. Burnout isn't a clinical diagnosis, right? It's a phenomenon. But you take a bunch of people who are altruists and perfectionists and have the same baseline predisposition to mental illness as the rest of the population. And then you put them in 'jail' for five years, and you script everything they do, right? You limit their sleep, you limit their food intake, you cut them off from their loved ones; they kill a few people by accident and you tell them everything is their fault, but if they keep their mouths shut maybe nobody has to know what they did. But in return, they have to take over running the prison. Do it to the next generation."

"Well, this is a little dystopian." Roy takes off his glasses, then puts them back on again, like he can't make up his mind whether he actually needs them. He gestures towards the main building, points in the general direction of the Zendo. "It does beg the question, why are we here? So many of us?"

"Did you expect medicine to feel like a life sentence?" I kick a patch of grass with my toe, lifting it off the earth. "Aren't you sick of living the way we've been living, Roy? Wouldn't you like things to change?"

"What's your life in a sentence? Sum it up."

"That's gimmicky."

"Shouldn't it be easy for you to come up with one if you're a writer?"

"I told you I'm a failed writer."

"Bad sentence. Plus I already told you, you're not a failed writer."

"That wasn't my *sentence*. Just please stop calling me a writer. I have to publish something real first. Otherwise I sound like an even bigger joke."

He touches my wrist. It's a surprisingly intimate gesture for a man I've just met. His fingers are weightless on my skin.

"You're not a joke," he says quietly.

I don't answer him.

"What's going on there?" Roy points at the grass I've excavated with my foot. "Looks like a biopsy."

"It's dirt, all right."

He bites his lower lip. Usually only women do that. This endears him to me. I feel his willingness to be vulnerable, the fresh bruise on his heart.

"Blue-haired internist," he says somberly, "I'd like to talk to you again."

"All right, man with fibreglass pants, let's meet tomorrow."

"I'll find you," he says. "In the rain, in the forest, I'll find you."

"Give me my regards."

Roy smiles at me, a puzzled smile, the smile of someone who knows a secret you know too, before either of you has figured out what it is.

o o o

SUPPER IS ALREADY going on when we get back to the main hall. I'm tired and cold. I eat mindlessly by myself in a corner, not really tasting the food. I go back to my room. My clothes are damp. Dampness has infiltrated everything. I decide to get ready for bed.

The shower room is as impersonal as the bathrooms. There are no recognizable patterns on anything: no florals, no deer on the hand towels. A small white lump of soap, featureless, like the statue by the pond. Even the shower door is a milky plastic. Nothing reflects light.

I hang my things over the towel bar, undress, turn on the water. Steam fills the room. The air is thick and soothing. The soap smells like eucalyptus. I shampoo my hair, watching a thin stream of blue run down my body and into the drain.

It's funny, but I notice how dense the air is, notice as I stand under the hot water how happy my body is to receive it, notice what it feels like when I breathe in that warm air. Summer days at the lake and heat rising off the water like the back of a great animal. My children, playing in the sand. Building pointless labyrinths of castles. Starting again from scratch every afternoon.

I can rebuild.

I can't rebuild.

I turn the water off, pat myself dry with the towel, wrap it around my hair. I melt a little coconut oil into my face, brush my teeth, decide to go to bed early, because I'm tired from all this sitting and thinking and talking.

It was a surprise to find myself writing about Mr. Ripple, but I guess I knew he was in there somewhere. Just one more bad thing that happened. One more story I'm carrying, one more rock in a bag of rocks.

"What if this is all our practice?" Ron said earlier. It hovered in the room, a radical idea.

There was a long, electric pause.

"Our clinical practice?" someone asked hesitantly.

"Our true practice."

I sit on my single bed in the dim light of the table lamp, putting away my toothbrush, taking my nightgown out of the drawer, where it's folded like a uniform. Ron, are you seriously trying to suggest all the crap things that have happened in my life are my practice? The people I feel like I've killed are my *practice*? How are they supposed to feel about this? And what if I go through all this *practice* just to find I can't handle medicine anymore? That I'm too old? Too tired? Maybe even irrevocably broken in a way I don't even know how to articulate?

What would the point of all of it have been, if I quit now . . . to be a failed or an unpublished writer, or whatever Roy said I should start calling myself?

o o o

SOMETIMES PEOPLE ASK why so many doctors are writers. But maybe the question really should be, why do so many writers put themselves through the unmistakable hell of becoming doctors?

I started writing again after my second son was born. I'd been seriously ill when I was pregnant with him. I was admitted to the hospital where I worked, under my husband's last name so the students and residents wouldn't notice it was me in an isolation room, my white blood count so mysteriously low that I couldn't be with other patients on a general medical ward. As I packed my suitcase that morning, unsure whether I was going for a day, or a month, or what would happen next, I looked at the sleeping form of my first little boy, not even two, his cotton pyjamas stamped with blue cars, the gentle rise and fall of his chest. I sat back down on the bed, tears leaking from my eyes, and watched him breathing as if I'd never noticed the miracle of that pattern before, repeating, repeating, a loop, no beginning or end.

I checked into the hospital. People I worked with came to consult on me, sitting across from my hospital bed with worried looks. Listening to their words, hearing but not hearing. Numbers circling in my head. The white count. The platelets. The liver enzymes. The beta-HCG. Blue cars on white pyjamas. I couldn't sleep that night, in my room high above the inner city. The matrix of houses. Chain-link fences. Crumbling turrets. Open windows, even in the dead of winter. Smoke rising from a cigarette. A woman and a man and a snarling dog. Trying to make sense of it all. Seeing if I could find a single thread of narrative to link what was happening outside the window and what was going on here, inside, with my life. Promising the universe if things got better, if everything could just turn out all right, there was something I'd do differently, even though I wasn't sure what it was. Holding on to the words of one of the nurses who had come to give me fluids and draw more bloodwork, a kind, motherly Caribbean woman who murmured she was sure I was going to be fine as she slipped the needle into my vein.

The next day, my counts had risen. The worst was over. It was just a virus, temporarily stunning my bone marrow, now receding without fanfare. Unlike every other person on that cancer ward, I got to go home intact. Even if I lost the baby, a baby who wasn't even a baby at this point, who was just the idea of a baby, really, a macadamia nut in my womb—even if I did, I was still the luckiest woman of them all. Leaving, walking out, going back to my one very real little boy who barely knew I'd been gone. Like reading a letter with horrible news, only to look more closely and discover it was actually intended for somebody else.

But I didn't lose the macadamia nut. He grew and grew, and soon he had a heartbeat. Then he had a face, and arms, and legs. Then he had everything else, and after that, he had a name: Adam, God's first man.

That morning in the hospital, I had made a deal and meant to keep it. I wouldn't forget how I had been lifted up by the random benevolence of the universe. One beautiful child. No cancer. A husband I loved. A home by the edge of a park, a lawn that blurred into an acre of trees, where birds nested in the shrub outside my window, hatching their babies while I nursed mine, their calls eventually mingling with the little macadamia nut's soft, piercing cry. This time I'd notice it all. I'd be grateful. I'd write.

And yet. In the months that followed, I'd nurse the macadamia nut to sleep and sit staring into his perfect face and weep. I wept because I knew that no matter how tightly I held him, in less than a year we'd have to say the first of an endless string of goodbyes, and medicine would come back for me like a reaper, the way it showed up when I went back to work after my first son was born, taking me away from him physically but also psychologically, separating us like a barbed-wire fence. I cried because I loved him and didn't want yet another baby to have to come second. And I dreaded all the other imminent separations. Nursery school and preschool and other women comforting my children while the hospital took over every aspect of my life.

I asked myself over and over, with an increasing sense of panic, "What is my way out?" I didn't want to go back to the prison experiment.

Some things in my life were different than they'd been a few years earlier, when I was still a resident. I didn't have to sleep over in the hospital anymore; I took overnight call from my own bed, and there were weeks when I didn't look after patients at all. But the whole experience of training had changed me forever. Wherever my body was, my head was always at the hospital. And the truth is that every time that pager went off, as it did several times a night for about a fifth of the year, that single electronic note took me back to my formative medical years, the ones where every page could mean a nuisance or it could mean disaster. Or it took me back to other sudden awakenings, in the middle of the night years earlier. Kenny Rogers on the radio at 4 a.m. Wendy fallen out of bed on her way to the toilet. Shattered plate glass. A broken mirror. A towel rack pulled out of the wall, Wendy lying there unconscious. The fear of not knowing what you'd find in the seconds before you got to her.

Once, when I was in high school, I was supposed to be looking after her while my parents went for groceries. I was doing home-work and suddenly realized the house was eerily silent. I looked for her all over, my panic rising. I checked closets, bathtubs, the bottom of the stairs. Shouting her name, not a word of an answer. Frantic, crying, barely able to breathe. She had to be unconscious or dead somewhere in a corner. Then: I happened to look out the window. She was in the backyard. Somehow she had crawled down the stairs and dragged herself to the garden on her bum. She had picked five or six potatoes. She was washing them in the pond. In her pink tracksuit, propping herself up, baptizing each potato in the dirty water. She gave me a tremulous wave when she saw me running out.

Jilly! I found some potatoes!

All of it still there, replaying in my mind on an endless reel. I needed to write it all down. I had to record it somewhere. None of it ever really over. I had to bear witness to my own life.

Writing was always the thing on my mind at the end of the day, lying in bed and listening to the tree branches scrape against the gutter, thinking and thinking with a hint of desperation, and then, finally, writing, feverishly, trying to preserve everything I could after so much had been lost, convinced that somewhere there was a bigger story that would help me make sense of everything, if I could only find it.

o   o   o

I WAS HEAVILY influenced by another doctor writer. I don't even remember his name. In the years after she left the rural hospital with the head-injury unit that never materialized, but before we moved Wendy to her own house, a little wheelchair-friendly bungalow at 81 Falcon Crescent, she lived in a nursing home. At that home, somebody basically wrote in her records that she was a spoiled brat. I was in medical school by then, and my parents asked if I could read her chart. I came across these words in a typewritten consultation:

> *I gather from speaking to the nurses that this young lady was simply allowed to do whatever she wanted at home, which has led to a host of behavioural problems.*

The author was a physician, a specialist. He had never spoken to my parents. He had just talked to a nurse who didn't know anything about Wendy, or brain injuries, and suddenly, instead of cancer, Wendy's family became the origin of all her problems.

God, that *hurt*. That casual, inaccurate sentence, written in haste, taking a split second to put us and our whole life out on the curb with the rest of the trash. I knew I would never write like that. I would never forget that particular betrayal, how it felt, like a random mugging. When physicians write, we say we "take" a history. And then we do literally take it, a sacred object, the story of your life, and we hammer it with something blunt until it's depersonalized. Until everything sacred about you, all you've done and overcome and lived, is bashed into a single, simplified thread. You thought you were a professor of linguistics who overcame a childhood of dyslexia and the loss of a parent at an early age, but no, you're just the kidney stone, and, by the way, the chart says you're obese, and you drink too much.

Well, I can't write like that. I don't have one more word of it in me, one generic line to say that you struggle to pass urine, that or your father died of coronary artery disease when he was fifty-three. Fifty-three! That made you thirteen on the last night you ever saw him, when you rushed up the stairs to finish the latest volume of your latest comic in bed, reading urgently, grunting at him when he came to turn off the light, telling you it was late, there was school tomorrow. Defying him after the door was closed by turning on a book-light under the covers so you could finish up with Spider-Man.

You didn't go to school that next morning. You would never have another chance to tell him good night.

That was your true story. I've forgotten your name, but I'll remember that story until I die. It's one of the stories people tell me, one of the histories I take in a way that is different from those of a lot of other doctors I know. But then I'm left holding them. I don't know how to hold them lightly, don't know how to let them go.

I'm with that boy, under the covers, turning pages, when there's an unmistakable thud on the stairs, like the time the movers dropped our sofa on the way to the basement. Calling out for Dad. *Dad?* But there is only silence.

This is your story, but somewhere along the way it's one more that became entangled with mine. And now, here I am in a room at Chapin Mill, still holding it.

16

The Perfect World of Jillian Horton

I can't sleep tonight. Something about this stupid bed. It's comfortable but so narrow. The last time I slept in a single bed was in a hospital room. Is that where all this uneasiness is coming from? Or is it Ron and Mick, pushing us towards all the rooms in the house we sealed off long ago?

I put on my housecoat and slippers. I move through the dark halls, stepping on hardwood illuminated by occasional fingerprints of moonlight. I trace my way to the dining hall. It's open, airy. The ceilings are high, tables set in front of picture windows that face the stream and the mill. Nothing is visible out in the dark. I see my weird reflection in the closest thing at the Zen centre to a full-length mirror: the window. There I am. Ghost-like. Shapeless.

The music room is just on the other side of the dining hall. I pass the empty tables, push open the heavy door. There's a full-size grand piano, like a beast in the darkness. I fumble with the switch, turning on a single lamp in the corner. The piano illuminates. Tentatively, I reach towards it. A hand on its greater curvature. Is that even what it's called? That's what it would be called if it were an organ. Like, a human organ.

Just touch it for a while. That won't bother anybody. I pull the bench out, sit down at the keyboard. One finger on middle C. The key drops. The hammer hits the string. It makes the softest, muted sound. I put my foot on the sustain pedal, push down. The quivering of the strings. An eruption, like a muffled gunshot.

I notice my breath. Fast, shallow. It's weird that I'm here, looking like a high school play version of Lady Macbeth in an ugly nightgown that I just now notice literally has a piece of gum stuck on it.

It's after midnight. I won't wake anyone up. I won't do anything.

I won't do anything.

Words I've said to myself at other times. Reassurance. A hint of bitterness, a slick note of something awful at the bottom of a drink. As if I could. As if I even have that much agency in my own life.

Do I have that much agency in my own life?

I play the G above middle C. Do to sol. A perfect fifth.

What's it like to be perfect, Fifth?

Once, a headline in a newspaper, an article about me when my album came out: *THE PERFECT WORLD OF JILLIAN HORTON.*

It was my short-lived folk/pop music career, just after residency, the one I was naive enough to think could turn into anything more than a few months on the radio and low-paying gigs in places where I'd normally be scared to use the bathroom. Not only is Jillian Horton's world perfect, but so is Jillian. Well, all she has to do, as that kid in grade eight pointed out, is lose some weight. *Then* she would be perfect. Jillian Horton practises medicine *per-*

fectly when she is not tinkering perfectly at the piano, despite all those people she may or may not have killed; but that is why they call it a teaching hospital. Also, it turns out her family has a genetic condition called Lynch syndrome, which makes them more likely to get cancer. But don't worry, Jillian didn't get that gene, because she's perfect! Footnote: she has sister who had a CT scan of her brain showing she had no brain left, a sister with key parts of her neural network rearranged like Mr. Potato Head's face. That sister is just the faintest shadow, really, a beauty mark on the Perfect World of Jillian Horton.

That sister, my deepest scar. The origin of all the best parts of me.

I press the sustain pedal again: cataclysmic sound of all the strings releasing. The softest cacophony.

I could be back in Toronto right now, cowering on a pew in a hospital chapel, like when I was an intern on call. Sitting there in stunned, miserable silence. How many more hours? Minutes passing more slowly than the drip of a leaky faucet. Pager clipped to my waist, like a bomb that might explode any moment. Sometimes I'd play the old organ in the corner, flipping the coloured levers down, layering the sickly-sweet vibrato, writing my own music, singing as I blocked out chords.

Where's my knight in shining armour?
Shouldn't he be here by now?
How'd you like your happy-ever-after?
(Jeers and laughter)

And then I'd play Joni Mitchell, "Blue" or "A Case of You," the same two songs over and over, the pager vibrating at every tender moment, reminding me I didn't even have jurisdiction over these few minutes in the middle of the night. This was right around the time Joni released the "favourites" album, with her smoke-eroded, barking voice, not a hint of the sweet songbird of years past. Everything slowed down and gummed up, orchestra crawling through all those sensuous lines. I'd go home, pull down the blinds, put on that album, curl up in bed, fall asleep in my work clothes on top of sheets I hadn't changed in weeks. Sometimes I'd get woken up by parties at the row of frat houses across the street, would open the blinds to see lines of stumbling, inebriated young men—men who occasionally watched porn on the second floor, curtains wide open, screens fully visible from the street. Everything had a cotton-ball quality, like a lucid, alcohol-fuelled dream, the kind you have when you're not used to drinking but one night you don't give a damn and make a show of getting drunk in front of your friends to prove you're a bigger mess than they originally thought, but they don't want to make you uncomfortable by wondering out loud if you're all right, so they have the courtesy not to ask.

When I started writing after God's First Man was born, when I promised to give up the periodic starving and all the other dysfunction if I could just be all right, I managed to write a book. I said it was fiction. But somehow, in hiding behind that label, I watered down the most important part of the story. That my patients were real people. That the terrible things that happened to them couldn't be recast as tidy parables. That my sister wasn't a metaphor. That my training had disfigured me and done me real harm. Me, a real person, living real, lasting consequences of it, not a fake, triumphant heroine whose story would end with the last page. The fictional story of my life wasn't even fit for a Dubble

Bubble comic when I was done rearranging the panels. Because I couldn't write honestly about all the not-perfect things in my life, not just the Mr. Potato Head parts but also the Ugly Doll parts. The years of swimming the river to the Buddha-that's-not-a-Buddha-but-a-column-of-stone part. The periodic wish to slip under the brown water and never surface. The blue whale.

Dubble Bubble. I love how the spelling condescends to me on the wrapper. What was it one of my colleagues said to me, about the students? It's time for somebody else to be their *Mommie*. Spelling the word that way for the same reason the cereal box says *Froot Loops*. Because the froot is fake.

Why do we let other people decide what the truth is about us? That can't last forever, not if you're going to have children. I mean, you can still abdicate that responsibility to the kid in grade eight or the teacher in the schoolyard or whoever, but then you have to make a very conscious decision to put no effort into bursting out of that prison, to writing the real story of your life. Failing to do that work is putting yourself last in the worst possible way, condemning the little people who spilled out of your body to another generation of dysfunction, to a mother who will never really be able to give them the gift of her full attention, to a lifetime of wondering why they weren't enough for Mommy. Spelled right this time, because there's no substitute for the real thing. Nothing will ever come close to me, and really being there for them means dealing with my own issues, *really* dealing with them. Otherwise, the legacy of that conditional love will plague them like a chronic virus, one they'll never be able to get rid of. I *want* them to be able to get rid of it. I want them to have a good life.

Can *I* have a good life?

There it is again, that ripple of exquisite pain, that very tender spot, the part of the iceberg below the water, so much bigger than what the eye can see.

One night, years ago, as I was helping her get into her pyjamas, Wendy said to me: "I have nothing to look forward to."

"Oh, Wendy, you do!" I remember telling her, a lump already forming in my throat. "There'll be vacations, and concerts, and maybe you can go to Nashville someday, and maybe you could even get a cat or a dog."

Could you say that with a straight face, to a woman in her late twenties, without guilt throttling you as you remembered the moment? Hey, having a brain tumour sucks, but . . . you might get a cat!

She never got a cat, or a dog. Never got to go to Nashville. She got sicker, had more seizures, lost what was left of her vision and hearing, had endometrial cancer, once ended up on a ventilator because she aspirated a hot dog, had a refractory antibiotic-associated infection that pretty much finished her off. She developed dementia, probably from chronic traumatic encephalopathy, because she had fallen on her head so many times over the years, because she never remembered or believed or accepted that she couldn't walk, and would go head-first into everything. Walls, doors, furniture. Losing consciousness, cutting her scalp open, breaking her nose. Blood on the carpet. Holes in the wall. Nothing compared to the holes in our lives.

Wendy, you do! You have so much to look forward to.

I have a burst of longing to talk to Roy right now, to tell someone about this part of my life. I've taken the tiniest sip of the grief I used to get drunk on all those years ago, crying in the chapels. Then laughing ruefully in the dark. Drawing Joni's map of Canada in permanent pen on my hospital greens. Thinking to myself,

Nobody knows about any of this. Not even knowing what I meant by *this.*

I had a nightmare once, a dream that shocked me awake because it was like a sharp flavour, something pure and basic. My parents in a car, with Wendy, at the top of an enormous hill. The brakes failing. The car sliding backwards, down the hill. At the bottom of the hill, a cliff that ends in oblivion. I'm standing there at the bottom, watching the car as it plunges over the cliff. I wake up screaming, not because I couldn't save them. Screaming because I'm not in the car with them.

The psychiatrist said: "That doesn't sound like a dream."

Two children lived down the street from us. Twins. Something had gone wrong at their birth. One had cerebral palsy, the other was perfectly fine. One day my mother and I were out for a walk. She gestured towards their house. "I always think of what it's like for that child," my mother said, shaking her head. Yes, I nodded, relieved to be able to talk about it. Me too! That child, the one that got away, watching her sister suffer, struggling to eat and talk, throwing things in anger when she couldn't communicate, the deformed limbs and the slurred words, and that healthy child infected forever with guilt, thinking, *Why? Why wasn't it me?*

But before I could speak, my mother said, "I just imagine her watching that perfect version of herself, stuck in her wheelchair while her sister is running around and having a normal life."

She meant the other child. Of course she did. Who wouldn't see it from that point of view?

Do you even know how lucky you are? How many people had said that to me over the course of my life? Well-meaning teachers, friends, extended family, every time I won a prize, every time they thought about Wendy slumped over in her wheelchair, my brother in the mental hospital, Heather just barely scraping by, struggling to find her way. And me, dancing around with my Midas touch, winning an increasingly absurd array of prizes, the perennial collector of good fortune. All those people clucking their tongues and shaking their heads. How could one child have so much and the others so little? How could anyone miss that disparity? Wonderful things were always happening to me. But just to *me*. Never to my family.

I did know how lucky I was. That was the problem. I didn't *want* to be that lucky if that luck set me apart from them. I didn't want to be apart from them. I wanted to be in that car, even if it was going over a cliff.

I just wanted to be with my family.

THREE

Shattered But Still Whole

We start at 6:30 again today. The windowpanes behind Ron and the others are black, opaque. Shoes come off outside the Zendo. Doctors shuffle in. One after another, we arrive, padding into the room in sock feet, finding a place to settle. We take our seats on raised cushions in total silence. It's damp again here this morning. Lots of wool sweaters, a few commandeered blankets.

I ease onto a circular cushion. Jodie is on the sidelines this time, back in her straitjacket. She looks deep in meditation.

Roy is sitting on a cushion near the back. His arms are crossed. The blanket over his shoulders only makes him look more bat-like.

After a long silence, Mick says, "Notice what arises."

My sister.

She arises, her face, her slack jaw, her scratched-raw, lolling eye. A current passes through me. A damp, private rush of emotion, involuntary, like a bodily function.

This morning when I brushed my teeth in the bathroom without a mirror, I turned towards the windowpane and raised the blinds, needing to see a trace of myself, even if nothing but shapes and light were reflected in the glass. And there she was, or rather, there I was, my aging face hiding in the shadows of my memory of her.

"Notice where the mind goes, and then gently bring it back to this moment. The present moment, unfolding."

Unfolding. Better than unravelling.

Am I unravelling?

Ravelling?

Must involve a lot of listening to Ravel.

Oh, that one G major concerto! A memory of the first few bars zings through me like an arrow. That summer at music camp, that one good July in Vermont when I was fourteen, lingering on the border between childhood and adulthood. Every corner seeping music. Hanna playing that concerto, Hanna who, like me, really believed she'd be a concert pianist, who had a breakdown a few years later and is now a "Reiki Master" with her own Wikipedia page that is very light on details.

Greg sneaks in. Late for Zendo! Weakling! Creeping in front of me, shifting his weight on the balls of his feet, cartoonish, as if that will make him less visible.

Feet have balls.

Feet don't have balls.

Jingle balls.

"Notice what arises. Come back to the breath."

Come back, breath.

What's wrong with me? How bloody hard can it be to centre?

Why am I always trying to escape?

What would I be trying to escape?

Vestiges of the self.

The inadequate self. The self that will inevitably make egregious errors, the self that will be like every other doctor. The self that is like every other doctor.

The self that watched that car go over the edge, everybody else still trapped inside.

Damnit. I notice my mind has wandered—not just into the backyard but through several lanes of traffic and to an airport, where it appears to have boarded a transatlantic flight.

Mick is talking, but it might as well be Sanskrit. He lost me. Or I lost him. He's saying something about a book. A book about healing yourself. What does he mean, healing? Crystals and stuff? Is this the come-to-Jesus moment?

He reads a short story about a sculptor who had an amputation. The sculptor made a sphere out of stone. Then he smashed it and put it back together with bolts and cement. It's in a gallery somewhere. It's called "Shattered But Still Whole."*

Mick, I'm getting annoyed with the mixed messages. That just confused me more. I'm holding contradictory truths, all right—like a jewel-encrusted stick of dynamite. Am I shattered, or am I still whole?

Or possibly I'm an asshole?

Ron's voice. Time for a body scan.

CT? That's a lot of radiation.

"Starting with the right foot."

What's this? Why are we starting with the foot, a vehicle?

"Noticing the sensations in the foot."

---

* Saki Santorelli, *Heal Thy Self: Lessons on Mindfulness in Medicine* (New York: Bell Tower, 2000).

My foot has a bigger repertoire of sensation than some men I've dated, Ron.

"Then turning our attention towards the ankle."

Ankle. I've taken you for granted all these years, except when you were the weak link after that bike accident. Strong work these last forty-four years, ankle. Seriously. I'm proud of you.

"If you notice your mind wandering, bring it back to your ankle."

If? Ron, my mind is a fucking sheep with dementia. My mind is a stray dog in a city of a thousand Dumpsters.

I look normal, though. I look the same as anyone else here, except for the blue hair. Maybe I am the same as anyone else here.

Maybe this is normal. Maybe this is most brains. Maybe everyone is here for the exact same reason.

What is that reason?

What is my way?

". . . noticing your right thigh."

Oh, *please.* Ron. Are you kidding me? That's the difference between me and you. My whole life I've noticed that thigh. Unlike the right ankle, which has thrived under my reign of neglect, the right thigh has managed to survive despite my constant scrutiny. *Why are you shaped like that? What's your problem? You're pretty smart, thigh, just lose some weight.*

This is exhausting.

Not sitting here on the cushion, but spending all this silent time with myself. With this shattered still-hole in my head. Listening to this relentless stand-up comedy audition. It isn't funny anymore. I'm kind of tired of it. No wonder I've dabbled in high-level escapism.

Light's breaking in the strip of windows that run around the edge of the Zendo. The gentle brush of dawn, the mildest, barely-there yellow.

Morning has broken.

Who sings that?

"Noticing the left foot."

The tingly, sleepy, buzzing left foot. The foot suddenly dis-embodied. Floating on the cushion. Weightless, like a water lily. Held up by everything and nothing. Motionless.

I notice my foot. I just noticed it.

Mine is the something.

Cat Stevens.

Cat's in the cradle. Blue boy. Blue hair. Blue whale.

When am I going home?

Saturday, actually.

Home. That word. Like in *The Wind in the Willows*: Mole, with Rat, walking past his abandoned burrow, catching a sudden, unmistakable whiff of his forgotten life, overcome by that most primal of memories, tears clogging his throat as he tries to explain it. *Dulce Domum.* Sweet Home. It's my home.

But it's not *home* that lands the winning punch today. It's "Little Boy Blue." How many years ago did Wendy write that poem, one finger at a time, commandeering her old Underwood type-writer, the one with the ribbon that always did something mad-dening just when you thought you had it in place, the tiny silver letters momentarily pinning it to the paper. That unbelievably painstaking staccato coming out of her room until the early hours of the morning, Wendy hunched in the half-light, her face only a few inches away from the keys. How long did it take her to write

Little Boy Blue, come blow your whistle
The sheep's in the corn, the cow's on a thistle
Where's the old man to break up the fight?
He's under the haystack, flying his kite.

How could I ever make a person who never knew her under-stand what a triumph it was for her, in that shattered body, on that old typewriter, to write those words? What would I give right now for one more glimpse of her in that chair, at that old desk, bathed in incandescent light? My little big sister.

Shattered but still whole.

I'm not noticing my face or my foot or my thigh anymore. I'm just struggling to breathe, to keep my composure, to not burst into tears in the middle of this Zendo.

What if.

What if Wendy never had a brain tumour.

What if I just keep noticing my breath. If I didn't unload a machine gun at every metaphorical duck that passed overhead.

What if I just strung those breaths together, one after another, each breath a unit of being alive? Would my life get better if I could do that?

If I stopped raging against suffering?

Or stopped bargaining with suffering? For it to end?

Ron just asked me to notice the face. This means I missed my pelvis and abdomen, my right and left arm, my back, assorted other bits. I'm like a game of hangman. Parts of me may never get filled in, depending on how this all turns out.

But I *notice* my face. The way it's lifted up, as if straining towards the light could bring me closer to her, my big little sister.

I'm sorry, Mick, but this is bringing me too close to that step, the one you said I didn't want to take. And it isn't just about whether I want to take it. You can't just walk on air because you want to. If you're going somewhere, especially somewhere diffi-cult, there has to be something beneath you.

Tell me how to take that step, genius. Tell me how I make it across that river in one piece. Tell me how you could possibly know there's enough time for me to start *close in*.

I ran out of time, Mick. I took too long. I didn't help her. I couldn't help her. It didn't matter that I swam across the river, because it was all for nothing. My sister is dead. She died last year. She was fifty-two. She died in her sleep. The Gambler was right: it *was* the best she could hope for. When I say I notice her here, what I'm really noticing is her absence. No blankets in a thread-bare room. An unlit fire in the chimney. A home without children. Noticing is ripping my guts out and painting *Guernica* with them, if you absolutely must know. But do tell me how noticing my damn ankle is going to make that any better.

Although it does occur to me, just as he rings a very large bell, as that gong quivers like a cartoon assailant's frying pan: he *never* said it would make anything better.

Failure to Cope

Roy comes and sits across from me at breakfast. I'm happy to see him, middle-school-cafeteria-happy. His bowl is ridiculously overfilled with oatmeal. He's topped it with dried cranberries, a deluge of milk. Red cranberries, little dehydrated rubies.

"Good morning, Blue," he says as he pushes his chair in.

What did he say he was, a radiologist? He has a psychiatrist's gaze.

"How was your morning?"

"Uneventful."

"Ha." He takes a fast drink of coffee, leaning forward and puffing out his lips when it goes down either too quickly or into the wrong passageway. I hand him a glass of water. He reaches for it brusquely, taking a long, emphatic drink. He wipes the back of his hand on his sleeve.

"Well, now you've saved me twice." He tucks his chin down, looks at me over the top of his eyeglasses. "Thanks for that."

I have a tray full of runny scrambled egg, toast I've cut into rectangles and layered with something from a Mason jar that looked like rhubarb or stewed reeds. Coffee in a white mug, where cream is settling into layers.

"Tell me about the first time I saved you."

He uses his spoon to make a crater in the top of his oatmeal. Then he fixes me with his gaze, dribbling some of the milk and berries on the table in front of him, because he isn't paying enough attention to his bowl.

"I think you know it had to be yesterday."

"I thought maybe it was in a past life."

"Yesterday's past too." Roy spills some milk down the front of his pullover. "Dang," he says, but makes no move to blot off the milk.

"So how did I save you yesterday?"

As soon as I've asked, something ugly occurs to me. What was he going to do? Hold his breath and walk into a duck pond?

Roy is still watching me intently. A few seconds pass, seconds of the sustained eye contact I'm only used to from *M*A*S*H*, where people look at each other for longer than ever actually occurs in real life.

"I was thinking of going home."

Home! Not planning on walking into a duck pond or putting a gun in his mouth.

"Are you serious?"

"Dead serious."

"Why would you have left early?"

"Listen, Blue." He pushes his tray to the side. "I'm a radiologist." He puts his elbows on the table, folds his arms and leans in towards me. "*I'm* the one who holds people up to the light."

"What light?"

"The lightbox."

"We don't use those anymore."

"It's a metaphor." He grunts. "You said you were a writer."

"I don't know if I said that."

"You did. And you have to know that absolutely *everything* is metaphor." He leans in and takes off his glasses. Again, that light brush of the fingers across the back of my hand. The tapping of his finger pads on my knuckles, as if he is percussing for an organ that accidentally ended up there.

"Metaphor is transfer," he says quietly. "We're always trans-ferring."

Does he really mean transference? Love, displaced, unex-pressed, longed for, moved from one shareholder to another. Or negative transference: all the things you could never give to the people you love, because they weren't capable of holding those things. So you passed them to somebody else. Even if it meant you would never be able to look at that person again without wincing, without recoiling at the memory of the exchange. Maybe even coming to hate that person, because it's safe to give them your hatred too.

"Metaphor is transferring *meaning*," he says, but he sounds less certain than he did a second ago.

My meaning, the one I inferred, feels more apropos. Because, in a funny way, I'm having transference towards him right now. It's amorphous, difficult to pin down or localize. But I feel it. An ache in my chest, a desire to play a role, to mime a part for him. To make a cryptic diagram of my wounds, to make him guess where they are. So he would look at me with the same undivided attention as a film on the lightbox.

That's all I wanted. That kind of attention.

All I ever wanted.

Roy raises an eyebrow. "You know we don't start silence until later?"

"I'm just thinking about what you said."

"I thought it might be a seizure."

"I barely slept last night."

"Why is that?"

"I don't know."

"Is that normal for you?"

"What are you, taking my history?"

"Fine, I'll go right to scanning your head."

"Yeah, because I really need to get a brain tumour from your radiation."

"They're rare."

"Not that rare."

"Rare enough."

"My sister had one."

"Oh," he says. "I'm so sorry." He puts his spoon down. "Did she . . . survive?"

"She did."

"So what does she do now?"

There is a long pause. How is it possible that Dr. Queen of Zendo one-liners has nothing on standby for the most predictable script?

"She's dead," I tell him. The word splits open the space between us, a meat cleaver emoji.

"Oh, wow," he says.

Now I'm on his lightbox. Held up, scrutinized. Is that what I wanted? No, I don't want it anymore. I want him to finish his stupid oatmeal and leave me alone. I want to go back to the emotional rock I've been living under. All this trying to figure out why I'm here is so much work. No wonder I put it off for twenty years.

He pours still water into his hot coffee. I watch him testing it gingerly with a finger before he takes another sip.

"Do you think we'd talk to each other like this if we worked together?" I ask him.

He looks surprised by my question. He pulls his bottom lip out with his thumb and index finger, like he wants me to inspect his gums.

"I don't think our worlds would collide." He takes another sip of coffee. "Which is really too bad."

"Why is that?"

"I like colliding with you."

An involuntary giggle rises from me. He's ridiculous, like those commercials of kids slurping cereal wearing Dad's suit. But then I have that vision of him eating ramen noodles and Costco profiteroles out of a bucket while he watches PBS, his face mottled by the TV's blue light, and I feel sad and sorry and kindly disposed towards him. I've met a lot of men like Roy. At work, everybody knows who they are, but at home, they're strangers. Fathers who don't know their sons and daughters. Men who are irrelevant to their wives. Tourists in their own lives.

"Your jokes are like from another century."

"I was born in one. I believe you were too."

I push my plate away. Roy is studying me, an unreadable look on his face. There's a strange absence of pretense.

"Were you really going to leave yesterday?"

"Yes," he says solemnly. "Because I hadn't connected with any-one."

"There are a lot of people here to connect with."

He pauses. He waits a long time to speak. At first, I think it's because he's being a drama queen. But then I see the emotion on his face.

"You know why I'm really here?" Another long pause. Now I'm holding him up on the lightbox, waiting for the diagnosis to reveal itself. "I think I have failure to cope, Jill."

I let out a big sigh. We sit at the table, eyes locked, people coming and going around us.

Roy looks at his hands in his lap.

"What are you thinking about?"

"Someone else who had it," he says quietly. "Someone who didn't survive."

A Time Roy Was Sure He Killed Someone, but Didn't

By Roy S., as told to Jill H.

Roy was a resident in a radiology program at a big American Hospital. He was just starting his third year. Morale was very low. By low I mean subterranean. Third year was when the radiology residents ended their pure clinical rotations and only did radiology. It was very competitive. There were ten residents in Roy's year, and they were starting to turn on one another like the kids in *Lord of the Flies*.

The radiology service at the hospital was absolutely massive. If you were assigned to the chest X-ray reading desk, you might look at one every ten minutes on a bad day, and then you had to report them. It often worked out to well over fifty chest X-rays a day. On the days when he was allowed to go home to his own bed, Roy would close his eyes and see the outlines of rib cages, illuminated, like thick white prison bars. On the rare occasions when he walked out of the building and it was still daytime, the real light from the sun would blind him. He took to wearing sunglasses and covering his arms just before he left, as if he were afraid of the light, or as if his skin were too fragile to withstand it.

The residents in his program mostly kept to themselves. Of the other nine, Roy only really knew two of them well. Sally was a tall, round-faced girl with a bowl haircut, from New York City. The staff radiologists tended to give her a hard time, because they didn't think as a woman she was up to the job, even though Sally knew more than any of the others. The other resident was Brian Yue. Roy didn't know anything about him, except he was from California and had scored the highest marks in his graduating class. Roy forgets how he knew that; it might have been from Sally.

Brian was friendlier than most of the other guys, and he never seemed to be trying to make himself look good at other people's expense, which was unusual. Roy liked him. Sometimes they grabbed soup and sandwiches together in the cafeteria. Brian always said he had a headache, swiping at his eyes like a kid who just woke up from a nap, because all that light and dark could be hell on your eyes.

It's hard to put a finger on when people start to change. Roy agrees when I say it's like the story of my children walking out into Lake Winnipeg as far as they can. It's not always clear they're in too deep when you watch them from the shore. Sometimes it's only clear after their heads slip under the water, and if you're standing on the shore watching, by then it's too late.

As their third year progressed, Brian became more withdrawn. Roy would ask him to go to the cafeteria, but Brian would stay in front of those huge lightboxes in the reading room. Roy heard a rumour that some staff were saying Brian was too slow. One staff member grumbled to Roy that Brian should go back to helping his parents make egg rolls, because he was missing so many diagnoses.

Roy regrets that he laughed at that joke. He wants me to know that on the list of regrets he has about his entire life, not including paying more attention to his marriage, his second-biggest regret is that he didn't tell the staff doctor Brian was his friend, his comments were racist, and he was an asshole.

One day, Roy walked into the reading room. He was looking for a folder of films he'd left on one of the desks. Brian was sitting in front of the lightbox. There were no films on it. He was staring at the lit panels.

Roy said, "What are you doing, trying to set your eyes on fire?"

Brian didn't answer him at first. He was rocking the tiniest bit in his chair, moving rhythmically, as if he were listening to music.

"Brian?" Roy said uncertainly. "Hey, you okay?"

"I'm fine," said Brian.

This moment is Roy's biggest regret. Roy wishes he had pulled up a chair. He wishes he had sat down next to Brian and asked him what was bothering him. He wishes he'd gone to get Sally, who was nicer, and warmer, and had a better way with words.

Instead Roy just said, "You should go home on time today."

"Soon," Brian said to him.

Roy found his stack of films in the corner and left.

That was on a Friday. Roy had the weekend off, a prospect he'd been savouring for days. He planned to sleep in on

Saturday, then go shoot hoops with one of the surgery residents who lived in his building, then do his laundry with a thermos of coffee, sitting on a beach chair by the coin-operated machines, smelling heat and bleach and fabric softener and catching up on his reading.

Saturday came, and it was exactly as he'd planned, except at night he went out with the friend who played basketball and they drank too much and stayed out too late, and so the next day Roy didn't even open his eyes until close to noon, when the sound of his phone ringing woke him from a deep sleep. He fumbled for the receiver on his bedside table, disoriented, rolling over on his freshly washed sheets.

"Roy, it's Sally." She was crying.

He could hardly understand what she was saying. Something about Brian. Something about the river behind the hospital parking garage. Something about Brian not swimming, and a security guard who saw the whole thing. Roy couldn't piece it together, not yet. His brain still wasn't working.

Then it clicked, the sickening truth illuminating, as with the flick of a switch. Brian staring at the lightbox. Brian going under the water, in too deep, nobody realizing it until his head disappeared under the surface. Everybody thinking he'd come up for air any minute. Even though by then it was already too late.

I sit with my face propped on my hands, watching the dining room empty out around us.

"You know what I've wondered, over the years?" Roy says after a long pause. "Why him and not me?" Roy's voice cracks, and he pauses for a moment. "That day when I saw him . . . I just wish I had done something."

We sit across from each other at the polished table while the light reflects onto it, his last bit of oatmeal long since gone cold. We look at each other for a long time. He must have downloaded it and read it last night, because he mouths one mournful, deliberate word.

Differently.

19

Washing the Bowl

ailure to cope. It sounds like a hashtag, not a diagnosis. Yet it's
what we're taught to write on the charts of people with cancer pain that hasn't been adequately managed, or elderly men
who are mixing up the twenty medications that eight different
physicians have prescribed for them in the last sixteen months.
It's pretty judgmental, something that girl in my graduate program might have said to me when she thought my plan to go to
medical school had me tied with Quixote.

It's particularly cruel when the thing we say you failed to cope
with isn't a hangnail but your own imminent mortality. How will
any of us cope when that moment arises? And is it failure to cope
if you drink to get through the worst years of your life or take
drugs to suppress memories of abuse or trauma that refuse to go
back in the box?

What does it even mean to cope? My mom managed to keep
us all clothed and fed. My dad showed up at work every day no

matter how broken he felt inside. It might have looked like we were all coping, but everything seemed so fragile, like it hung from a filament that could never bear the weight of all it carried, the love, the entanglement, the grief and injustice. We were in a desperate state. There wasn't much between us and that cliff in my dream, the one I sometimes wanted to plunge over with my family.

A story my dad told me: when my brother descended abruptly into psychosis as a teenager, when he was seeing animals in his empty closet and convinced that someone had poisoned him, when the regular hospital said the only place he could be helped or managed was a psychiatric facility, one weekday morning Dad took him there, for "assessment and treatment," both of which would turn out to last for the next twenty years. He coaxed him inside the front entrance, my brother trembling and afraid. He gave the clerk at the front desk my brother's name. They were expecting him.

My poor brother was crying; he didn't want to go. Dad told him he needed help. But before he had the chance to say anything else, two men appeared, just like in the movies. Each took one of my brother's arms, and they dragged him screaming through two large doors that locked behind him, his cries eventually fading into silence.

My dad taught at a community college. He had to go to work that day. He went to work no matter what was going on in our lives.

That morning, on the way to his office, Dad ran into his boss in the hallway. A close talker, a man who always punched everybody in the arm and massaged their shoulders and shouted motivational platitudes.

"Having a good day, Bob?" He slapped him on the back. "C'mon, smile, man! Aren't ya having a good day?"

They stood at the top of a staircase.

Dad said in his whole life, he had never come so close to hurting someone, to grabbing his boss and throwing him down the stairs. That moment, forever preserved in his memory, the scene so real to him in retrospect that he sometimes wondered if he'd actually done it.

He told his boss his day was going fine.

He walked away.

So what does it mean to say you're coping? It's what I'm thinking about as I leave Roy at the table, fill my mug with coffee, stop in my threadbare room to pick up the schedule for the rest of the day. Is coping doing what you have to do to get the job done? Or is it about something more than hauling yourself through misery? And how do we determine how much any one of us can take?

o o o

"'You DO NOT *have to be good*.'"

"That's a relief."

"Stick a sock in it, Jodie."

"Everyone heard her talking to me like that, right?"

Greg points at me. "'*You do not have to be good*.'" He stops. "Actually, you two do have to be good, or I'm not going to finish 'Wild Geese.'"

Jodie rolls her eyes at him. "We'll behave ourselves."

You do not have to be good.
You do not have to walk on your knees
for a hundred miles through the desert, repenting.
You only have to let the soft animal of your body
    love what it loves.

Tell me about despair, yours, and I will tell you mine.
Meanwhile the world goes on.
Meanwhile the sun and the clear pebbles of the rain
are moving across the landscapes,
over the prairies and the deep trees,
the mountains and the rivers.
Meanwhile the wild geese, high in the clean blue air,
are heading home again.
Whoever you are, no matter how lonely,
the world offers itself to your imagination,
calls to you like the wild geese, harsh and exciting—
over and over announcing your place
in the family of things. *

Joss leans back against the wall. God, she is effortlessly cool. Her blond hair drops in front of her face like a window blind.

"That line . . . *'the soft animal of your body.'"*

Jodie puts her fingers on her lips, makes a kissing gesture. *"Magnifico."*

My children. Skin smooth as soapstone. Their little rib cages, arms above their heads, tussling with pyjama shirts. Orange soap and lavender oil. The clean, simple lines of their small forms.

Greg turns to me. "What do you think that bit is about walking on your knees?"

"Why'd you ask *her?*" Jodie's irritated. "I think she's the least likely of the four of us to have done that."

I stick my tongue out at her.

Joss's vintage necklace is no less excellent today than it was

---

* Mary Oliver, "Wild Geese," in *Dream Work* (New York: Grove/Atlantic, 1986).

yesterday morning. She has a cup of tea in a mug she must have brought from home that says *Bernie Sanders Was Right About Everything*. She pulses the bag into her cup, finally lifts it out, dripping tea all over the floor.

"Why do you think they chose this poem?" she says.

"You're dripping," Jodie warns her. "They chose this poem because we *have* to be good."

I correct her. "We have to be *perfect*."

"Obviously not possible."

Greg is milking his goatee again. "Where did that idea even come from? Like, that you have to be perfect at a *hard* job?"

Joss likes this point. She wags her finger at Greg. "You know, that's brilliant. Like, you have to be perfect doing the *hardest* job . . . shouldn't the hardest job have the lowest expectation of perfection and vice versa?"

"Yeah, like, 'Make my coffee perfectly.'"

"No one joke about perfect coffee."

"By the way, I heard somebody smuggled in a French press."

"Find out who. I'm transferring to that group."

"Even making perfect coffee is a way to practise, right?" Jodie likes this tangent; she's excited. "Have you heard this Zen thing, 'Wash your bowl'?" We shake our heads, no. "The student asks the master, 'How can I become a master like you?' And he says, 'You like to eat breakfast?' Student says, 'Yes.' Master says, 'So wash your bowl.'"

Joss's not buying it. "That's a bullshit story."

"How so?"

"Condescending."

Jodie shakes her head defiantly. "Totally disagree!"

"If a monk talked to me like that, I'd kick him in the nuts."

I wave a hand between them as if they're about to brawl. "Guys, you're both right. There's wisdom in it, *and* it's condescending if the person who's saying it thinks they're better than you. Like all the doctors from another era telling us how much worse they had it, but meanwhile they had like ten treatments to choose from and couldn't have imagined anything as evil as a bad electronic health record."

"That's exactly what I meant," Joss says, placated. "As if our generation are all slackers."

"Oh God, but the students *today*!" Greg's hand moves from his goatee to his temple. "They're a mess. They want it all, and you can't have it all."

"Okay, wait, but isn't that what our teachers said about us?"

"Yeah, but we didn't want it *all*. I didn't anyway. I just didn't want my life to feel like a bomb went off in the middle of it."

"Man, no kidding." Joss parts the hair in front of her face, revealing a deep frown. "My life is a serious shitshow."

"So, *tell me about your despair*."

"Fuck off, Jodie."

Jodie sits up straight, looks affronted. "I want to hear it!"

Joss pauses. She pulls her knees to her chest. "Medicine tore me to pieces."

"In what way?"

She laughs ruefully. "In what way did it not tear me up? That's the shorter list."

"Okay, let's hear that list."

"Well," Joss says. She doesn't seem able to decide whether she wants to hold her tea or put it down.

Greg sniffs. "Is that green tea?"

"It's, like, an oolong or something."

Jodie presses her. "The list."

The tea is set down on the hardwood. Joss crosses her legs, props her elbows on her knees, lets her chin rest on the back of her hands.

"You know how after strokes people get hemiparesis and they don't recognize some part of their body, right? 'Alien hand' syndrome?"

Jodie lets her hand float up towards my face in slow motion, preparing to strangle me.

"I told a shrink I had alien life syndrome." She shakes her head. "Like, is this my *life*?"

Greg is nodding like a madman. "Yes. *Yes*. Or, like, is real life only when you're in the hospital?"

"I've thought that too."

"One day on the way home from a shift where I had to pronounce a teenager dead from meningitis, I walk by this lady screaming on her porch." I shake my head at the memory. "I run over to her ready to, you know, protect her from an assailant, and she's like, *'Somebody stole my fucking bike!'* And I'm like, 'I thought it was an emergency,' and she gets in my face and screams like a poltergeist, *'It IS an emergency!'*"

"It's like we're constantly shuttling between two planets. I read that somewhere."

"I don't want to be all geeked out, but isn't that kind of what the poem is about? Like this line." Greg squints at the handout, clears his throat. *"Meanwhile the world goes on."*

"After the ecstasy, the laundry."

"We think we're so terminally unique." Jodie shakes her head wistfully. "Like we're just uniquely screwed."

"Why would we be different from every other person on earth?"

Greg interjects: "This is what she's saying in the very last line! *'No matter how lonely, the world offers itself to your imagination, calls to you like the wild geese . . .'*"

"Calls to me like my pager going off over and over . . ."

"*'Harsh and exciting . . .'*"

"Isn't anybody else here lonely?" Jodie looks at us expectantly. "I mean, didn't medicine make you lonely?"

"Or sick and crazy?"

"Or dead inside like zombies?"

"Order!" Jodie pounds her fist like a gavel.

"One problem with this place is zombies need flesh foods."

"Oh, fuck. How is a person supposed to get anything done around here?"

"We don't have to be good! The poem said so!"

Laughter. Joss's mug tips over. The remnants of her oolong spill onto a cushion. Greg and I put our arms in the air like zombies and start shuffling towards Jodie on our haunches.

I notice something, a feeling in my chest. Lightness. Joy. Or something that tastes like it. That flicker you get, of a déjà vu. A place you were once, even though you can't say where or when.

I used to feel like this. Some parts of training were good. Besides Joni Mitchell and the chapel and crying by the lockers, and the crushing despondency, there was also laughter. Laughter with my friends. Fake-paging each other to call the morgue or the gift shop, writing prank consults for our crushes and our enemies. Endless jokes about the staff doctors and their idiosyncrasies. Holiday shifts dressed like elves. The patient who asked if he could borrow my phone to call my friend, his doctor, so he could tell him he was an asshole. Laughing ourselves sick as schoolkids when a kind, dignified, elderly attending told us solemnly we should always remember that beer was a powerful vasodilator.

We drank a lot, probably too much. I suspect this is a scourge of more residency programs than is generally known. We drank to escape the constant fear of screwing up, to facilitate the laughter. We drank to let go of deep inhibition, the overdeveloped capacity for delayed gratification that so often epitomizes the medical personality. Sometimes we drank to find connection with one another in short, futile affairs. In a state of chronic sleep deprivation and ongoing high-grade stress, we looked for comfort in places we wouldn't normally go to find it. We made a lot of mistakes at work, then those mistakes spilled over into our personal lives. Doomed relationships, failed marriages, the long, humiliating tail of flings we never would have had if we were really in our right minds.

But Joss and the others have reminded me that I used to laugh more. With colleagues, with patients. Belly-laughing to the point of tears. The elderly woman who told me she lived with a granddaughter who called her "the cockblocker," because young men were creeped out by the idea of sleeping over at her grandma's, me so surprised to hear these words come out of her mouth that I nearly fell out of my chair, her laughing so hard I had to turn up her oxygen. The funny gifts from patients, our little inside jokes. The humour I developed reflexively, growing up in a home where there was a cloying sadness, where the bridges from crisis to crisis were short and unsteady. What a crucial skill, to be able to make people laugh on those bridges, lifting everyone up, higher, away from the water. The one thing I can still do when there is nothing else to be done.

The bell in the hall rings. We won't get to hear the rest of Joss's list. I don't think we have to, though. We all know what's on it.

That's why we're here.

20

Get Out of the House

Mick brings us all into formation in the great hall. He starts by asking how everyone is doing. People call out words. *Anxious. Rested. Excited. Impatient.* I giggle to myself. Roy, a few seats over, catches my eye, raises an eyebrow. I mouth the joke: *Inpatient.* He doesn't catch it. He puts on his glasses.

"What?"

"Forget it, I'll tell you later."

Mick's wearing a black tracksuit. He looks like he's going to rap at a funeral. He puts up a slide. *When things go wrong.* The energy in the room changes. A slight, perceptible shift.

We all have these cases. The saying is that every surgeon has a graveyard. People who stalk us our whole lives. Things we often can't speak about, because we're supposed to be perfect. Also, because people might sue us. And because of shame.

Mick puts up a bunch of numbers we've all heard before. How many of us will make mistakes, how many of us will struggle as a result. After a complaint, a doctor's already elevated baseline risk of suicide will increase five-fold.

A lot of medical errors are thinking problems, but most don't have their root in negligence or incompetence. We're easily swayed by external influences. A colleague tells you a patient has pneumonia. Because you like and trust him, you ignore the nagging voice in your head protesting that there isn't much evidence for pneumonia, and the next day the patient has a massive pulmonary embolism. Or a patient with a history of addiction comes into the emergency department with confusion. Nobody does a spinal tap, because someone has written in the chart that confusion is how this woman presents when she's high. Later, she dies of meningitis, a diagnosis you never even considered. Or you think a patient has a rare disease; you work him up, you tell your residents, you say to every consultant, "I'm sure this will turn out to be sarcoid." But when the evidence mounts that it isn't sarcoid, or whatever uncommon disease you've hung your hat on, your mind can't change lanes. You've invested too much. These are cognitive errors. Our brains get stuck in one gear.

But there are other reasons we make errors. Inexperience when we're young. Fatigue. A system that constantly asks us to play the odds that most people won't die if we only skim the surface of their history. Pressure to look after more and more patients whose problems are increasingly complex. New and cumbersome electronic systems dumped on us with increasing frequency and too little training, more paperwork, more regulations, threats of repercussion if we don't comply with having email addresses affiliated with each clinic or hospital where we work, requiring us to sift through piles of duplicate messages sent each day to our multiple accounts. And more expectations that we expand *our* services to become the solution to a reduction in resident work hours, we who are still under-slept and under-resourced and doing the most we can with what we have, and frequently have no more to give to anyone, we who ourselves are struggling with grotesque rates of burnout, addiction, depression, suicide. People like me, here for all the right reasons, people who have loved this profession and believed in it with our whole hearts, and have been brought to our knees by it.

Mick is setting up an exercise. He asks us to find a partner. I'm really not into this right now. I don't feel up to walking a stranger through my personal cryo-preservation unit of people whose names I will remember until I die, or at least remember until I am very old with severe dementia looking after one of those rubber baby dolls in the nursing home.

There's a young woman I haven't met before, sitting to my right. She's wearing a shapeless brown knit dress that looks like a tuque with armholes. She has asphalt-black hair pulled into a bun at the nape of her neck. While I'm eyeing the body toque and wondering if she knitted it herself, she turns to me.

"Partners?"

I nod, unconvinced. I had designs on Joss. I don't feel like getting to know any more strangers. Especially strangers who look young enough to be crying in my office or complaining that I haven't referred them to cooking classes in a timely manner. I'm tired. I want to build a cushion nest in a space under one of the windows where there's a patch of sunlight and go to sleep. Why don't they let us sleep more here, anyway? Why do we finish every night at nine and start meditating before the sun is even up? I thought this was going to be a retreat. Do I feel better? I don't think I feel better.

The woman's nametag says "Ikiru," and that she's a senior surgical resident. She has a round face that reminds me of a kewpie doll, with heavy green eyeshadow and a lot of eyeliner, and a small tattoo of a butterfly with one wing on the back of her neck. I noticed it in one of the other sessions. In my head I tried out a joke to Jodie and Greg about the parlour running low on ink, and then another joke about it being a koan. She has a pierced eyebrow.

I would never have come to a retreat like this when I was her age. There weren't any retreats like this then. I might even have thought it was presumptuous. It took me twenty years to end up here. Why should she get to fast-track? I had to graze a certain kind of rock bottom, over and over, just quick communes with stones before resurfacing, before I became aware that spending so much time at the bottom wasn't normal. When I was her age, I coped by spending hours jogging through the downtown core until I coughed up mucus streaked with car exhaust. Sometimes I was post-call, and I'd sprint in a state of delirium. Laughing at my own private jokes, the sound of my laboured breathing masking the turmoil in my body, the way you might turn up the radio to drown out something terrible going on in an adjacent apartment. Sometimes a streetcar would glide by me, silver rails appearing behind it like columns of mercury as it retreated into the distance, and I would think, *It could have hit me. I would have been fine with it hitting me.*

Then I wouldn't have to go to work tomorrow.

Did Ikiru go through all that too? Even if she did, she hasn't proved she can choke down another fifteen years of it. Is she going to try to tell me she knows what it feels like to do this for half your life? Please. She hasn't driven this car long enough to know how it handles on the road.

Mick is talking about deep listening. Oh, God—really, Mick?

My entire day is spent listening. And then talking and wondering if anyone is listening. And then going home, where, granted, it's possible that I don't always listen.

Okay, maybe even that I rarely listen. Because by that point there's nothing left.

Mick gives the instructions. *Pause, relax, open.* Talk in such a way that the conversation flows, without interruption. Pick up on what your partner says. Follow, like a piece of music. Respond to one another, be responsive. And listen, really listen.

Ikiru is looking at me out of the corner of her eye. She hops out of her chair onto a cushion. The large group begins dissolving into pairs, seeking corners, distance from others.

"Where are you from?"

She tilts her chin, looks at me with annoyance. "America."

Ikiru, don't go there with me. We're at a conference. That's not what I meant, and I know you know it.

"Yes, I meant where in America? Don't you have fifty states?"

"California."

I notice that her shirt dress has a hole in it.

"There's a hole in your dress."

"It's part of the design."

She wrinkles up her nose. Is that an evil smile? What is that mean thing she just did with her face?

Mick rings a bell. Wait a minute, Mick. I don't want to talk to this girl for the next hour of my life. She's glowering at me from beneath a pierced eyebrow—and I'm sorry, Ikiru, but as a surgeon you should know that an eyebrow is not meant to have a hole in it. I think I detect the slightest upward curl of her lip. She hates me. Maybe I'm too geriatric for her. My boots are real leather, not vegan. My hair dye isn't environmentally friendly.

Is this her judging me or me judging me? Well, it doesn't matter. I'm not opening up to this girl.

There's silence, between us, not particularly pleasant, a weak current of uncertain energy. The silence of a stand-off.

"I'll talk first," she says finally, reluctantly. She shimmies on her cushion so we're a few inches closer to each other.

Mick asks us to sit in silence for a moment. To notice what's present before we begin to speak. I notice my irritation, the drama unfolding in my mind, the tension I'm writing between me and this stranger. It isn't her fault, any of it, what happened to me at the school. Most of my students were good kids, and maybe she's good too. Maybe she's blaming me right now for an internist who yelled at her on the phone some night when she was trying to decide whether to anti-coagulate a post-operative patient with chest pain. I'm noticing you, anger. Where have I read that anger is a response to helplessness? All the rage we can't express, or feel powerless to express? Wallpapering a water-stained wall, ignoring the leak.

The bell rings. Everyone waits until the note is gone, the long tail of its decay over. Ikiru takes a sharp breath. She puts a hand over her tattoo.

"So this is about a man with a nasogastric tube." Her hand moves to the hole in her sweater. She traces its outline, probing it the way I imagine she might search a wound for foreign bodies.

"It was on the surgical ward, and I was an intern. I was on with a fellow who told me not to call him for anything unless I thought a patient had to go to the OR." She takes in another tight breath. "The patient was around eighty. He was really dignified; he had been a college professor or something. Just a really nice man. Like a bookish grandpa. He had a mass in his stomach, and we were

196

trying to fatten him up a bit with feeding before we removed it. There wasn't much else wrong with him. So, one night on call, I had to put the tube in through his nose, and it was really difficult. I don't know why. He kept gagging, and then he was spitting up a lot of blood, and after five tries, the nurses were rolling their eyes and telling me to call the senior. But I couldn't. This senior, I don't even think he would have come, and if he did, he would have ripped me to shreds in front of the whole ward." She looks down at her lap. "I mean, as I tell you this story, I guess I could have, but the thing is I *felt* like I couldn't."

Silence. The words Mick left on the screen: *pause, relax, open.* I'm not relaxed. I'm with Ikiru, on the ward, trying to slide that tube into the right nostril while the patient gags and convulses, while the exasperated nurse rolls her eyes at my uselessness.

"So, finally, I'm able to advance it, and we tape it into place. He settles, the nurse cleans him up, we get an X-ray. And I look at this X-ray, and there's a nasogastric tube right where it should be, in the tip of the stomach. So I order his feeds. At a low rate. Just twenty an hour. A trickle, right? It's after midnight. I don't think I've eaten since lunch, but now at least one of us is getting fed."

Pause, relax, open. As she's telling me the story, I feel myself opening to her. Inhabiting the exhaustion. The stifling uncertainty, the chronic anxiety about what could happen next.

"I went to do something else. Write orders, see somebody with post-op pain, I don't remember. But I got a page after a couple of hours that the patient with the NG tube was in respiratory distress. I go see him, and his lips are blue. Fingertips are blue. He's working really hard to breathe. His O_2 sat is 70, and he wasn't even on oxygen before. That same nurse who was looking at me like I was a pile of garbage, she has her stethoscope over the right lung and says it's all crackles. So I call for an X-ray, and I try giving him some diuretic in case he's in heart failure. I have this feeling of total panic. Like, is he having a heart attack? His blood pressure's good. It doesn't make any sense. So I get another X-ray, right, and I go to look at it."

Ikiru pauses. She folds her hands behind her neck, the way you are supposed to if the police tell you to come out with your hands up.

"His right lung is full of fluid. Can you guess what else is in his right lung?"

I pause, trying to follow what went wrong. "How could it be the nasogastric tube? You looked at the X-ray."

"No, I looked at *an* X-ray." Her hands release, slide down the front of her chest, as if she's wiping off residue. "I looked at *another* patient's X-ray. A patient with the same last name, five rooms over. And that patient's NG tube was correctly placed in his stomach. Unlike my patient, whose NG tube was positioned pretty much in his right middle lobe. And we filled that lobe with 20 millilitres of feeds an hour. And he proceeded to develop respiratory failure, and we couldn't get his oxygen levels up, and within an hour he was intubated on a ventilator in the ICU, and a couple days later he went into cardiac arrest and died."

I watch her face carefully. There's something about the tone of her voice, as if she's testifying in front of a jury. A faraway quality, narrating while she watches these events unfolding on a little TV screen in her mind. Her testimony doesn't matter. Whatever the jury finds, Ikiru will always think she's guilty.

Something similar happened to me once, and the memory of total helplessness washes over me. One mishap after another: a sudden, unexpected movement during a procedure, a needle gone slightly astray, a lung punctured instead of a vessel, a chest tube inserted with complications. A meeting, with an elderly man and his three children, a painful discussion about what to do next for their mother, his wife. That man, holding my hand at the end of the meeting, squeezing it with both of his, looking at me squarely, his cloudy eyes filling with tears. "I know you did your best, dear." Holding me with so much grace. How could he do that when my best at that moment had been inept? That kindness, so undeserved, so lacking in understanding of my transgressions. That unbearable kindness, alcohol on an open wound. He gave forgiveness. Total and complete forgiveness. Did I deserve it?

Do I deserve it?

But it's not the time to share my own war stories. I pause, relax, open, listen deeply. I don't interrupt Ikiru, the way I normally would at this point in the conversation, turning the spotlight back from her to me, the way most of us do. I sit with her, just listening, nodding my head. Meeting her gaze.

"And the thing is," she says, and now her voice thickens, her words becoming slow and deliberate. "My mother had just died. It was my first week back after her funeral, and nobody even knew."

My mouth opens. My hand flutters to my sternum, her words hurting my heart.

"Oh, Ikiru! I'm so sorry."

"It's okay. This is almost five years ago now, right?"

"Oh, I know. But your *mother*." Suddenly I see it all differently. Her eyebrow piercing, her weird sweater dress, her air of indifference, all gestures of uncertainty. Manifestations of rage cloaked as indifference, a grief that fills your own lungs with something as heavy as concrete until you're sure you can't live another minute. This is a girl who lost her mother. A girl who is still grieving, who will be grieving intermittently for the rest of her life.

"How did she die?"

"She was sick for a long time." Her breathing is slower now, her voice calm. "She had a brain tumour, actually."

A brain tumour. Words that slice me along an invisible plane, words that seem to trace back to my own mythology, the meaning of my life.

"That's a strange coincidence," I tell her, circumventing pause/relax/open, emotion drawing out each of my words. "My sister had a brain tumour."

"Oh, wow." Ikiru meets my gaze now. She pauses, without relaxing. Then she says, with trepidation, "Is she okay?"

"No, she's dead too."

"Oh, wow," she says again. "How old was she?"

"She was fifty-two."

"Did she have kids?"

"No. She had the tumour when she was a child. It kind of wrecked everything. Like, our entire lives. It's your turn to talk, though. I need to be listening."

"Obviously you are listening," she says, with the slightest note of annoyance. "I'm talking like this *because* you're listening."

"So what happened to your mom?"

"She had a seizure. This was, like, when I was in med school. Then she had surgery when they found the tumour. It completely wrecked her personality."

"What kind of tumour?"

"Anaplastic astrocytoma."

"That's what my sister had."

"That's weird."

"Yeah."

I pause. I have one of those moments where you become sus-
picious of a series of too-perfect coincidences and think maybe
everything around you is a screenplay. People you're meeting
for the first time suddenly seem like extras from an earlier act.
The whole thing so coincidental, it could just be a clever Netflix
pilot.

"It's funny, because my sister was on my mind this morning,
in the Zendo."

Ikiru is staring at me now. "I was having the same experience.
It was just as if my mom died yesterday."

"Like she was there in the darkness."

"Exactly what was happening to me."

"My sister used to wear this brace on her leg. Did you notice
that guy, Steve, wears one?

He was sitting right in front of me."

"I didn't notice."

"I was thinking to myself"—here my voice catches, and the
words pile up in my throat and I don't know if I'll be able to extract
them—"I was just thinking, what was the point of that brace anyway?"

"Which one?"

"My sister's. She was never going to walk again. So why go
through that every day? The special sock? The special shoe?
And then the brace? Like, it was pointless. And sometimes she
didn't want it, and she'd fight it, and my mom and dad would
go through all the work of getting this brace on and off every
single day, or else her staff would." Now the words are literally
choking me, and because Mick and Ron keep making the same

point about noticing what you feel from one moment to the next, I notice the tension gathering in my face, the air pressing up against my eyes. "It was totally hopeless, right? The best outcome was like in 'The Gambler.' You know, Kenny Rogers? The country singer."

"What happens in 'The Gambler'?"

"You just hope you die while you're asleep."

"Oh, fuck, yes," says Ikiru.

"And that's what happened to my sister. She died in her sleep. How'd your mom die?"

Ikiru wipes a hand across her eyes, smudging her sparkling green shadow. I can't tell if she's crying.

"She was in palliative care at the end. She didn't even know me for almost a year. She made no sense. We used to say her last meal was a word salad."

I stifle a laugh. Someone in another group looks over at us. I cover my face.

"Love the black humour."

"No other kind."

"Did that resident you were working with ever find out your mom died a few weeks earlier?"

"If he did, he never said anything."

"Did you think about telling him?"

Ikiru looks at the back of her hand, notices more smudges of eyeshadow. She traces them with a long, delicate finger. A surgeon's hand.

"Actually, I'll tell you something, but you'll think I'm a horrible person."

"I doubt it."

"I heard his dad died. Maybe two years after that. I saw him in the hall. He looked really shitty, shittier than usual. I was going to say something to him, but he walked right by me and looked through me, like I wasn't even a person. And I just thought to myself, Now it's your turn."

"*Schadenfreude.*"

"Yeah. Ugly, though. It's not like I wished his dad would die."

"But you hope he learned from it, right? Like, maybe it made him more human."

"I think the only thing that would make that guy more human is a personality transplant."

"Why do you think he acts like that?"

"Somebody told me once he used to be a really nice guy, everybody in his med school class liked him, that he always joked around. But he started to change during residency. By the time he was a fellow, he treated everybody like dog shit."

"I don't think I buy that he started out that nice. Although it is classic Stanford Prison Experiment."

"I'm split on it too. Except, do you think women just direct more of that stuff inward? Because it's unacceptable to behave like an asshole if you're a woman, right? But all that rage has to go somewhere. I mean, I'd never be an asshole to a patient under any circumstances."

"But you'd be one to yourself."

"Yep."

Is that why she has a pierced eyebrow and a hole in her sweater? Is that why 80 percent of what I ate for two years was almonds and black coffee? *Jill, we've traced the call. It's coming from inside the house.*

"I feel like this is a really important idea."

Get out of the house! Get out of the house!

"It's funny, because I kind of assumed you wouldn't even want to talk to me because you're older," she says, her voice sounding almost shy. "And then we have this huge thing in common."

"Which one?"

"Ha. I just wish my mom could have seen me graduate." Ikiru's voice is distant now.

I'm picturing her walking across a stage in her cap and gown. Her father, maybe some siblings somewhere in the audience. The emptiness of the moment as Ikiru reaches out to accept her degree from the chancellor, or the generic dean. Another name called before she is even finished pausing for the picture, a photo for which the university will charge her eighty-nine dollars, a photo she'll show her mother in her hospital room a few weeks later. When she points at her own unsmiling face and explains what's happening in the photo, her mother will gesture at the bald, round head of the chancellor and say a single word: *Egg*.

"There's always this void," I tell her. "Losing a mother is totally different—I wouldn't even presume to know. But in general, it's difficult not to focus on what's missing."

"I think about it like an amputation. It's kind of the inverse of the story Mick told about being shattered but still whole. You can still have a great life, a meaningful life, but you can't look at the situation and say there isn't something missing that used to be there. But then you find there are a lot of other people who have had amputations, and at least you don't feel alone."

"I completely get that."

"You know how I ended up doing this Zen Buddhism meditation stuff? It was a quote I read somewhere. 'The universe doesn't exist to make you happy.' For me that was a tiny lightbulb moment. None of this is personal."

I have the feeling I'm looking in a mirror, the way it some-times used to be with the students. Like I'm handing a letter to a younger version of myself, like I've come to this place in order to tell that version of me something I wish I could have heard then.

"This is really weird, okay? But I have to tell you. I wrote this song once. It's kind of exactly what you just said."

"You write music?"

"I used to, but then it kind of died on the table."

"Well, that's not okay."

I pick up a pen. I write down the words for her in my note-book. I tear the sheet out, and she takes it from my hand.

There should have been birthdays and nephews and nieces
Instead of these shards of a life torn to pieces but

Life doesn't owe us anything
Life never owed you anything
Life never owed me
Anything

She reads it twice. "This is *exactly* what I meant. Like, life never actually failed to do what it said it would do, because it never said it would do *anything*."

"Because it's just a construct that it made a deal with us."

"It lets the hurt just be hurt."

"Manslaughter instead of murder one."

"Can I keep this?"

"Sure."

"Will you play this for me someday?"

"You can't afford me."

It's the first time I've really seen her smile. She has a beautiful, wide grin. Perfectly straight teeth. A vulnerability about her, a loveliness I missed when I was composing a narrative, the one that was only in my mind.

"Why do you have the piercing?"

"Why do you have blue hair?"

"Okay, but it doesn't hurt when you dye your hair."

"This didn't hurt much."

"But why choose anything that hurts?"

"It was kind of an impulse. People make assumptions about Asian girls, right? You're so nice, you're so polite, you're going to follow all the rules. You know about the culture of cuteness? *Kawaii*?"

"I thought that was a piano."

"A super cute piano."

"Maybe medicine needs more *kawaii*."

"No, medicine needs more of the last part. The *ai*."

"What does that mean?"

"Love. Or, like, *aisuru* is 'to love.'"

"That sounds like your name."

"Only the *-uru*. It's the verb."

"So what does 'Ikiru' mean?"

"There's a movie," she says, looking embarrassed. "My mom loved it. She had a background in film. It's black-and-white. I doubt you've heard of it. It's called *Ikiru*. Don't laugh if you think it's cheesy."

"I won't laugh."

"It means 'to live.'"

"You definitely have the best name of anybody here. Even if I'm going to withhold judgment on the eyebrow."

She rolls her eyes. "You sound like a mom."

The weight of those words fills the space between us. Our eyes meet. Now Ikiru's eyes really do fill with tears. They roll down her cheek, leaving trails.

"I *am* a mom. And your mom would be so proud of you."

"Well, I'm a sister, and your sister would be so proud of *you*."

"I don't know if she would be, actually." Here my voice catches, and I break her gaze. "She didn't have a chance to do all the things I did, and I've screwed up so much. I've wasted a lot of time. You never get that back."

"What would you have done differently?'

Now I'm the one wiping away tears. "I wouldn't have thrown myself under the bus for so many years."

"Like, how?"

"Like, just the way I treated myself during residency. I'd have been nicer to a dog."

She nods slowly, emphatically. Her voice is gentle. "What else?"

I drum a finger on the floor, thinking. "Probably joined Costco earlier."

She laughs out loud. "What is it with doctors and Costco?"

"So efficient."

"You're a crazy lady," she says, shaking her head. She wipes away her tears, punches me in the shoulder like we're old friends. "We don't get time back. But maybe going through all this teaches us how to spend it properly."

"Or what it's actually worth."

"Or both."

She gives me another shy smile. "I'm glad we met."

"Me too."

Another long, drawn-out minute passes between us, the kind of space people rarely leave between one another.

Ron and Mick can't end this moment with a bell. It was always here, like a secret door you've been trying to kick in for years. And then, in the midst of this trial, as you hang your head in defeat, you notice that around your neck you are wearing a key.

Silence

For the rest of tonight, after a session with Ron and Mick, we'll be in silence. Supper is in silence. Evening meditation: silence. In the morning, we'll eat breakfast in silence.

But first we talk about silence. We talk about how it has many meanings for us. We have often experienced silence as punitive. A parent or lover who froze us out in anger. A teacher whose long, ominous pause before answering our question spoke to the depth of our shortcomings. The stunned silence of rooms where we've decimated lives with news of masses, failing bone marrows, the ominous results of scans.

Mick is giving us a "send-off." He says it might not be easy. That not everyone responds to silence in the same way. He tells us not to make eye contact with each other, that many people find it invasive in silence. We may notice the intensity of our own thoughts in ways we've been able to mitigate and dilute before. He says we'll need to sit with these things, just let them be.

Part of me bristles at these instructions. I've lived through tough things in my life. Mick's framing a period of silence as if it's learning to perform brain surgery. It feels pretentious, like he's making a big deal out of a tiny laceration.

But why do I bristle? What constitutes a problem in my universe? Well, brain surgery. It's not easy to compete with that. And yes, I know this definition is a form of extremis, and even a tiny laceration can become a life-threatening problem if you don't sew it up properly and watch for signs of infection and tend to those signs if they arise.

I catch Roy's eye. We look at each other for a long, quiet moment. Ikiru is still sitting next to me. I feel connected to her, as though a bright silver filament is fluttering in the air between us. I look around the room and locate Greg and Jodie and Joss. I'm going to miss talking to these people until tomorrow. I know more about them than I know about doctors I've worked with for the last decade, people whose offices are steps from my own. I'm not going to want to say goodbye to any of them on Saturday. I feel a curtain of anxiety come down over me, like I'm swimming at slow speed in very cold water. I don't usually notice these sensations, or these emotions. I just plod through the cold and the darkness, heart pounding, breath shallow. It hits me like a wave of sickness: I don't want to leave here. I want to see my children, my husband, my family, my friends, but I don't want to leave these people. I don't want to go back to the way things were before.

Do I have to go back to the way things were before?

The stillness in the room is electric. Fifty people, not speaking, breathing. Noticing.

I'm thinking of my children, how I loved them before they could speak. How their cries could tell me whether they were tired, or sad, or hungry, or wet, or afraid. Listening for different notes in their brief utterances, watching the way corners of mouths turned up or down, how eyes widened or closed. A look, a glance. A squirm, a particular kind of sigh. A song without words. I came to know what they needed. Even when they didn't know.

We sit in complete silence. Occasionally someone sniffles, or lifts a hand, wiping away tears. I turn my attention to my breath. Every time I notice my mind wandering, I try to come back to the temperature difference in my mouth and chest, cool air entering my warm body, lungs expanding. I notice how each breath displaces me, lifts me up higher on the cushion, nudges my shoulders and rib cage skyward. My mind still wanders. It never stays with the breath for more than a few seconds.

But maybe I can shepherd it back to the breath when it's only gone as far as the backyard. Maybe I don't need to let it get as far as the freeway, or the airport, and then I won't have to spend days walking back, retracing my steps to the place where I find my breath. Maybe this is a way to conserve energy, an alternative to holding court with everyone I know. Talking to Stan, Mr. Ripple, the Dutchman. The students. My parents. My sister. My friends, my enemies.

None of the people I talk to in my head are actually here. This seems so obvious, and yet it isn't obvious at all—that I spend half my waking life interacting with what are basically holograms I'm generating myself.

And what is it that I'm saying to them, trying to get them to understand?

Mick uses the mallet and strikes the metal bowl. The sound is a slow, resonant quiver.

211

The quality of the energy in the room changes. People stretch, yawn, sigh. We stack our cushions in the corner. It's getting dark outside, and our movements are reflected in the opaque glass.

Slowly, we form a silent procession up the stairs, our feet padding on the rug, our eyes cast down. We splinter at the top of the staircase, going our separate ways.

I wouldn't have imagined that you could get a group of fifty doctors to follow all these crazy rules. But here we are.

At the top of the stairs, despite the instructions, Roy looks me in the eye. I meet his gaze. It is mine to decipher. As with my children, I know he is asking me for something in that moment. I nod at him silently. I can hear the music in his head. A song, without words.

22

When You Walk Away

We meet by the blank deceitful Zen head, as if we had planned it. Roy's sitting on the bench, wood stained with dark rainwater, wearing his windbreaker and knee-high rubber boots.

"I wanted to talk to you," he says.

"I know."

"You didn't dress for the weather."

"Snow's my forte."

"I'll give you my windbreaker."

I sit down next to him. He takes it off, drapes it over my shoulders. We're under a massive tree with long, spidery tendrils. I didn't really notice it yesterday.

"I saw you talking to that Japanese girl."

"Ikiru."

"It looked intense."

"It was intense. Who were you talking to?"

"A psychiatrist from Northwestern."

"How was that?"

"Helpful. I told him to bill for it."

"What did you talk about?"

"A pregnant woman who died of a pulmonary embolism a few years ago. My resident misread the perfusion scan as normal, and she presented to another hospital in cardiac arrest."

"That's awful."

"The kind of case that makes you want to steer your car into a tree on the way home."

"I'll bet."

"What was your mistake?"

"We didn't get to it, actually. We ended up going sideways."

Roy turns to look at me. He's tall, with the perfect posture of a choir boy. There's a youthfulness about him. Vulnerability, a familiar sadness.

"You can tell me now if you want."

"It's too late."

"Why would it be too late?"

I put his windbreaker on, although I'd rather keep it draped over my shoulders because of the tenderness of the gesture. I've started to shiver, but I'm trying to hide it, because I don't want him to suggest that we go back inside.

"It wasn't really a medical error anyway."

"You let me tell you about Brian. Can't we hold it up to the lightbox together?"

"You really want to hear this now?"

Roy nods. I look down at the small drops of rain beading on the surface of his jacket. I feel a surge of something akin to love for him. Not romantic. An intimate kind of gratitude.

"His name was Michael."

"That's the angel of protection. Did you know that?"

"Well, he did a bad job for his namesake in this case. He had cystic fibrosis."

Roy lets out a heavy sigh. He knows cystic fibrosis the same way I do, as an insidious son-of-a-bitch assassin that slowly sucks the life out of young men and women before they reach forty. Condemning them to early death by suffocation, drowning in their own cement-like mucus, unless they submit to lung transplants: torturous, elaborate surgeries with no guarantees.

"He was my age. Just a kid, basically. He wanted to be a writer, Roy. Just like me. We met when I was an intern."

"How did you meet?"

"I was on the respirology service. He was a chronic inpatient, too sick to manage at home. It was December of my first year in Toronto. We rounded on him every day. He was weak as a kitten. He had these ugly glasses with a bar across them. The kind the guys wear now, because they're in fashion again. He had a penchant for T-shirts with slogans from old political campaigns. I remember he had one that was, like, *Nixon—he'll get the job done.* This kid's whole life was irony." I can see Mike's hair, shaggy, an involuntary mullet because of the energy it took for him to shuffle down to the hospital's hair salon. It catered to eighty-year-olds bound for long-term care. He told me once he was thinking about getting his hair set in curlers so he could experience a sense of belonging.

"He was listed for a transplant, and he'd waited for months. He kept getting infections, so he went on and off that list. But the way I really got to know him was the coffee shop. There was a Second Cup in the hospital lobby. Right by this big statue of the angel that we walked by every day. Mike would be down there when I was on call, playing solitaire. I'd always say hi. And then I started saying more than hi, because he'd be reading, and I wanted to know what he was reading. And I saw that he was reading stuff I loved. Like *Maus*. And weirder stuff, too, like Martin Amis. And within a couple of months we were talking every time I was on call and if I was at a different hospital, he'd send these great postcards to my home address. They were never about how he was doing. They were always about the stuff we'd talked about or full of questions about how *I* was doing, but nothing about him. I think he was so sick of talking about his body and how much mucus he had that day and cystic fibrosis that he just couldn't handle the spotlight being on him anymore. Except once in a while he'd say, 'My lungs are coming. I know it.' And I'd nod, even though I honestly wasn't sure he was going to live long enough to get them.

"So then I switched hospitals for my next rotation. I went to Toronto General. Sometimes we called it Toronto's Genitals, but it was a great place. Very new. Glass and high atriums and a couple of blocks from where insulin was discovered. I'd walk by Banting's bronze head, and sometimes I'd rub it for good luck. I know it's weird—don't laugh. My next rotation was Nephrology. I'd see everybody who was on dialysis for the whole hospital. It was crazy busy. Those people are *sick*, right? And I showed up on that service and saw the list of consults, and there was Mike's name. Post-transplant. He was in kidney failure, but it was improving, and he'd had a transplant. This was in the days before we all carried cell phones, so the whole thing was probably just too rushed for him to let me know. But I think he would have if he could have. I think I bridged two worlds he inhabited."

"Which two?"

"Life and death."

"That's what I thought you'd say. But there are others."

"Yes, like sick and healthy, right? So I went to see him after the transplant. He was really bloody ill. He was in the ICU, and he just looked like roadkill. They couldn't get him off the ventilator at first. His lungs looked good, but all this other stuff was going wrong, including with his kidneys. The way he looked at me, that first day, with the tube in his mouth and his eyes half open, I wasn't even sure if he knew I was there. He told me later it was the lowest point of his life. I didn't want to see him that way. I avoided his mom. I couldn't face her fear. Usually I could handle anything, but I couldn't even look at her. Mike's dad died when he was a kid. He had a heart attack. It was just the mom and Mike and another brother. I don't think they had anybody else. She clung to Mike."

"Maybe even the way your parents clung to your sister?"

"Yeah, maybe, Roy. Good pickup."

"Kind of obvious."

"Maybe to you. So Mike started to get better. Every week or so he made progress. He got up in a chair. He walked a bit. He made it out of the ICU. He slowly jettisoned all the gear that goes along with acute illness. Oxygen. Foley catheter. Central line. All that stuff. He had a birthday. I brought him a cake. It was stale, though. It's a dumb regret I have—I didn't go to a real bakery."

"That's a total Captain Sullenberger. 'How could I have landed the plane better?' You know . . . *Miracle on the Hudson*?"

"God, of course I know. He's one of my heroes."

"Sorry. What happened next?"

"He got discharged. He kept writing me postcards. We went out shopping together once in Chinatown. He had one of those old cameras where you develop the photos yourself in a darkroom.

217

He took a picture of me and sent it to me in the mail. I was in this old long plaid wool jacket I used to love, kind of the way I liked to picture myself, with the wind in my hair and my mouth open because I'm laughing."

Roy tucks his chin down. He looks at me skeptically. "Was he in love with you?"

"Oh! No, I really don't think so." I'm shivering now. The wind has picked up, and the surface of the pond is rough and pricked with little white waves.

"Well, were you in love with him?"

"Oh my God, no. Never with a patient. Gross." I blow on my fingertips, then rub my hands together like I'm trying to light a fire with them.

"I don't see what the problem was."

"There wasn't a problem."

Roy pauses. He looks at me for a long time before his gaze travels to the ground, then back up to my eyes.

"So where are we going with this?"

I'm holding my breath. Roy sees that I'm shivering.

He wants to go with me.

"Should we walk?" he asks. I nod. My teeth are chattering. "We can go inside if we have to."

"No, we can't, because it's silence and we're breaking it right now. Let me just tell you the rest of it. It's not long."

We stand up at the same time, our boots cemented into the wet mud. We extract them and walk, following a path that loops around the pond.

"Remember I said I didn't have a phone. But I had a pager."

"The box of pain."

"Yes."

"So several months go by. They're bad months. My sister is really sick. My parents are falling to pieces back home. I'm getting caught up in some really dysfunctional coping of my own. We don't need to get into it—I'll tell you about it another time. I'm really hitting a new low point, though. Just getting through the days, going through the motions, except everybody is telling me how great I'm doing. I'm kind of withdrawing from the world after I get home. Closing the blinds, watching movies and letting my machine take all my calls. I'm not calling my friends. I'm not responding to half my emails, and I haven't answered Mike's postcards for months. I'm a senior resident now, and I'm at another hospital. It's called The Western. And one day, out of the blue, I start getting these five-digit pages. I call back, and they're always these automated not-in-service numbers. Nobody there. And these calls keep coming, Roy. They happen every day for about three weeks. They make me crazy. I phone the Toronto Western switchboard, and I'm practically yelling at them to stop putting these calls through, right, because it's annoying and you're in the middle of seeing a patient and you keep wondering who's paging you and whether they're going to call you again. They say *they're* not paging me. And then one day they stop. I don't even notice for a few days that there haven't been any of the pages. It's like in *M*A*S*H.* where they always say, 'Do you hear that?' when they're in the OR and the shelling's over."

Roy and I come to the end of the path. We turn around, heading back to the faceless Buddha.

"You know it was him paging me, right?"

"I do. But why couldn't you answer the pages?"

"Because they were numbers you could only call from inside the hospital, where he was. Like when you call a business, and you have to dial the extension of the person you want to reach.

He was paging me to an extension. Just an extension, without a location. Like telling someone to call you at a local number without giving them the area code when you're in a different state. You can't answer the call from that other state without the area code. He wasn't a doctor. He wouldn't know how to call someone on a pager. Get it?"

"I think so," Roy says thoughtfully. "But why was he paging you?"

"Because he'd been readmitted. He'd gone back to work, gotten run down, and started having recurrent infections. He was just so hungry to live a normal life again and make up for lost time. He'd taken a trip to the U.S. with some friends. It was one of the last postcards I'd had from him before all of this. There was some fast-food restaurant he always wanted to go to, like an In-N-Out burger. He did it. That was the one pathetic dream he got to realize. A one-dollar shake. He was trying very hard to be normal."

"So what did he say when he got hold of you?"

We're back at the Buddha without a face. It's pouring raining now.

"He didn't get hold of me, Roy. The calls stopped because he died."

His voice is breathless, gentle. "Oh, Blue," he says. "How did you find out?"

"I was back on the respirology ward where we first met, seeing an internal medicine consult. And I said to one of the nurses I knew up there, 'Hey, I haven't heard from Mike in a couple of months. But we keep in touch, and last time I heard from him he was doing great!' And her face went white and she said, 'He had an overwhelming fungal infection. He just died.'"

Roy and I are standing next to the fake Buddha, like we're hovering over a gravesite. He puts his arm around my shoulder, gingerly, as if I might lose my balance and fall down the embankment. "I didn't even believe her. I thought it had to be a mistake, but she showed me the obituary. It was taped up onto a filing cabinet. I missed the funeral by two days."

Two days. The moment comes back to me. Mike is dead. His picture in the paper, above a few short paragraphs, the ones that could never do justice to him or his complexity or his short, difficult life.

"I don't know how I got through the rest of the day. I guess I went on autopilot. It's all a blur. On the subway I just kept thinking, *I have to get home. I have to get home.* And when I did, I fell onto the carpet and had one of those cries where you can't even move afterwards. I couldn't sleep that night. It was probably 2 a.m. when I figured it out. All those pages I couldn't answer: they were from him."

"What do you think he made of it all, Roy?" The question has a new urgency, an angle I haven't considered for years. "That I thought I was too big a deal to answer him?"

"I doubt that, Jill," he says with immense tenderness. "Nobody who knows you could think that."

"Why didn't I connect any of the dots?"

"You know why. Those dots just keep coming at you when you're a resident. You don't have time to brush your teeth. How could you have figured that out?"

"I should have."

"Is that a pattern, for you, that you berate yourself?"

"Isn't it a pattern for everybody here?"

"You know about the 'curse of knowledge,' right?"

"Of *course* I do. God, what do you think, Roy—I'm visiting from another planet?" He reclaims the arm he had around my shoulder. He must be cold in his thin shirt. "Let's go back in. You're soaking too."

"No, this is too important. So, the curse of knowledge is when we can't imagine other people not knowing what we know, because it's impossible to see as if *we* don't know, right? Our minds can't do that."

"I *know* what it is!"

"It hits the brakes on our compassion for other people when they make mistakes. We think, how could they do anything that stupid? But it also puts the brakes on *self*-compassion. An area where people like you and me don't tend to excel. Would you say that's right?" I don't answer him. I'm looking at the wet ground. I'm thinking about Mike. And Mike's voice. His jokes. That stack of postcards I never answered.

"The other thing is, Jill, something else you said struck me. You said at the start, 'He was just a kid.'"

"He was."

"And you said you were the same age."

"I did."

"That must mean you were just a kid too."

Roy, don't screw with me. I feel an ache in my chest, my breath coming faster and faster.

"Can we agree that it's not your fault?"

"I don't need that from you right now," I tell him, and I mean it. What does he think this is, *Good Will Hunting*?

There's a long hush between us, like we're in the Zendo. The main building glows in the distance, illuminated from within. It looks like it's part of a toy village.

After a while he asks me, "Since you keep erroneously tell-ing me you're a failed writer . . . I'm guessing you've read Joseph Campbell. *The Hero's Journey*?

"I have it in my office."

"Good, so you know where I'm going with this."

"With what?"

"Your arc. Your hero's journey."

"My 'arc'?" I can't help rolling my eyes at him. "Don't you think a person on a hero's journey should be an actual hero?"

"I think the greatest heroes are anti-heroes."

"Well, then you'll love me, Roy. I'm an anti-anti-hero."

"Double negative equals a positive. My point is just, you can move through all the stages, or you can get stuck in one. And maybe you're stuck in the third one. Do you remember what it is?"

I shake my head.

Roy pauses. "It's 'atonement.'" He looks at me for a long, quiet moment. "If you won't let yourself leave atonement, you're never going to get to the next stage. Do you remember what *that* is?"

No, I don't remember it either. I'm sick of the teaching ses-sion. I notice he's shivering now too.

"It's the journey home."

There's a long pause.

I start unzipping his windbreaker to give it back to him. It's too much. I'm too much. Roy's too much. Fuck him. Fuck all these weirdos, except maybe Jodie and Greg and Ikiru and Joss. This feels like some kind of fucking Care Bear cult.

Roy makes a *tsk* sound, the way he did the first time we spoke, when he admonished me for saying he was crazy. "Why are you taking that off?"

I thrust his coat towards him. My eyes are filling with tears, and there's nothing I can do to stop them. I want to go inside.

"Maybe you don't think things are allowed to get better for you, for some reason," he says gently. "Or maybe you don't want to go home?"

This is the most weirdly accurate thing anyone I barely know has ever said to me. What's weirder is how it affects me, like a band tightening around my heart. A visceral, reflexive pain, like when you cut yourself. I'm temporarily overcome with a desire to pretend I don't know what he's talking about, to tell him he's mistaken me for somebody else, a person with another kind of past.

I don't want to go home. A sudden, guilt-ridden flashback to the time I read my sister Heather's journal. I found it in her bedroom. I was just a bratty teenager, rummaging through her things while she was out, only looking for pocket change or fodder for low-grade blackmail. She was eight years older than me—a lifetime, really, at that age. She'd saved all the money she'd earned waiting tables at the university cafeteria, taken a trip to California, come home with a diary with a picture of the ocean on it. I'd seen it sticking out of her backpack, and I intended to plunder its secrets. I ran that journal to my bedroom and hid under the covers, cackling to myself, expecting to find lists of boys she liked or the name of the ABBA member she wanted to marry. Instead, a handful of grief-stricken lines.

I don't want to go home. I feel like a terrible person for saying it because things are so hard for Mom and Dad, but I wish I could never go back. There's nothing there for me. Nothing.

I stared at the words.

224

The dawning, in that moment. How much we were all suffering, privately, pretending we were fine. How brutally difficult it was, living with Wendy, caring for Wendy, grieving for Wendy and everything we'd lost as a family, my brother seemingly vanished off the face of the earth. How it consumed my parents, totally, how their own lives and dreams were shoved to the side, how they somehow managed to plod through indescribable conditions for decades. How Wendy's needs always *had* to be at the centre of everything. How profoundly, how biblically she *suffered*. How her illness was a wildfire that tore across all of our lives, how there was nothing we could do to stop it. How hard it was to say that *I* suffered. How hard it still is, to say that.

Maybe I surrounded myself with the sickest people I could find so I would *never* have to say that, so there would always be somebody around me who was suffering more. So I could minimize my own problems for the rest of my life.

It was an impossible situation. And it was nobody's fault. Even the doctors who had been awful, even in light of how awful they had been. They were products of a sick environment.

It wasn't their fault.

What did Don Henry, my old piano teacher, say to me all those years ago, when I was trying to decide between Oxford and medical school? How could I not have thought of it before now, his choice of words? He said I should remember that it was okay for me to want a good life for myself too, that I was *entitled* to a good life. That you have to live for yourself and not just for everybody else. I guess I must have looked stricken, because he said he felt as if he had said something terrible to me or misspoken. I hurried home from my lesson that day, something I couldn't name boiling up inside me.

After we stand in silence for a few minutes, Roy asks, "Why do you say you're an anti-anti-hero, anyway?"

"I was supposed to save my family."

"From what?"

"I don't know."

"Were you supposed to go back in time?"

"I didn't have a plan, Roy. It's not literal."

"But your guilt is literal."

"I'm sure yours is too. What about your friend Brian?"

He pauses. I hear him take a breath, and as he does, I notice my own breathing, cold air moving into my mouth and throat, rain matting our hair, rain leaving fleeting craters in the surface of the pond, our arms and legs stiffening in the cold. Light is just giving way to dark, dusk settling on top of the forest. I'm shivering hard now; I can barely feel my fingers.

"Roy, do you think the problem is we're holding ourselves responsible for things that aren't our fault? Or is the problem that we need to forgive ourselves for the things that actually are our fault?"

"What do *you* think?"

"About you or me?"

"Whatever's true for one of us has to be true for both of us." Roy puts his arm around me and steers me back towards the main building. "For everybody in there. Every one of us."

○   ○   ○

WE PART WAYS at the top of the stairs, keep our eyes to the ground. A few people are out walking in the rain by themselves, on the bridge or headed down towards the mill. No one seems to have noticed us together, talking, flouting the rules.

I head to my room, wet clothes sticking on me. I peel them off, change into sweatpants and a fleece, get under the covers, see if my teeth will stop chattering.

I've noticed a shift. I'm not raging against being here anymore. There's just an immense feeling of sadness, a sense I've been totally defeated. I try to follow that emotion like a trail of breadcrumbs, hoping it will lead me back to its origin. As if going there enough times could unlock a way for me to write another ending. But an ending to what? My un-hero's journey? The students, turning on me, coming at me with pitchforks? Mr. Ripple screaming he'd never forgive me, Mike not being able to reach me before he died, the twenty-four-year-old woman on the cardiology ward, that very first cell mutating in Wendy's head, the pie-graph doctor yelling at my mom and dad? My brain, stuck in a groove like a damaged record, repeating the same things over and over. Saying to me: maybe if I went back one more time, just *one* more, the ending might be different. As if there really were a solution, to any of it, a way to put shattered-but-still-whole back together again.

Mick keeps asking, *What's present for you right now?*

It's that I'll never stop being who I am, never stop practising with love, or going down into the mineshaft when others are trapped there, so I can be with them. I *love* being a doctor. You wouldn't know it when I talk about what it's done to me, but you'd see it immediately in the way I practise. I know who I am when I put that stethoscope around my neck. I know why I'm there. My patients know why I'm there too. They see me, the way van Gogh saw Gachet and painted him as fully human. That's not where things went wrong.

It's that I thought—I really thought—if I were a teacher, or an associate dean, maybe a dean someday, I could just teach people to be themselves. To be *human*. To make it so no one would ever scream at the parents of another little girl with cancer again.

But teaching isn't a job for one person. You can't do it alone, without some kind of infrastructure, something behind you and underneath you that won't break and send you tumbling over the edge the first time somebody stabs it with a pitchfork. I started walking through the fire thinking I could change everything. That just my faith would be enough. Now I'm the one who needs a teacher, to show me the way through the fire.

What would Mick or Ron ask if they were here right now?

What if you accept this fire? What if there is no fire? What does it mean to walk "away"?

Well, I'm not the Gambler; I'm not walking away. I'm looking *for* my way. I started this week, with my first step, the one I didn't want to take.

I came here.

Mirroring

We fumble through a silent supper. I try to chew and taste my food, but it's impossible to keep from thinking about everything Roy and I talked about by the pond. I like the way Roy listens. I like the way his too-bushy eyebrows are always moving, like the silhouette of a far-off seagull. I see him over by the window, alone with his head down, eating a flesh-less chickpea patty with a very large glass of milk, chewing like a schnauzer. God, what an endearing weirdo. I wish I was sitting with him. Just as I'm considering whether to leave my table for his, Ikiru appears from behind me. Wordlessly, she joins me. We don't make eye contact. But I *feel* her. It's as if we're radiating benevolence towards each other. I soak it in for a few minutes. I notice Roy drink his milk in one long inhalation. He pushes his chair away abruptly, stands up, takes his tray to the big, morgue-like sinks in the kitchen, dumps his scraps into the compost bin.

As much as the silence is unsettling, I have to admit it's also a relief. I feel constantly responsible for everybody. This is a problem that tends to afflict women more than men, because we *are* assigned responsibility for everybody. There's literature to show that patients expect female physicians to spend more time with them than male physicians. That we have to be even kinder than men in order to not be judged harshly. So much effort funnelled into being pleasantly innocuous, lest we be told what most of us are told at critical junctures at some point during our development: that we are too much. And then, shortly thereafter, that we are not enough.

This on one of my high school report cards:

Jillian works very hard to be creative, but she needs to put more effort into having this occur naturally.

There's not a Zendo tonight. We're gathering outside, on the large, interior courtyard, for some kind of silent meditation. Ron has told everybody to dress warmly. I slip into my rainboots and short black raincoat, like I'm planning on blending into the night. Everyone is waiting by the sliding glass doors that lead out onto the raised deck. There's a feeling of expectancy, of some looming drama or catharsis.

Greg is standing next to me. I stifle the instinct to say "hi" because of the silence. A smile dies on my face in a bad impression of the *Mona Lisa*. Why haven't we looked at that painting? What do we think about that look on *her* face, anyway?

Mick ushers us into the courtyard, starts calling out orders. It's like a morose square dance. We start by finding a place on the deck, facing outward. Then he tells us to turn towards the person on our right and follow them in a slow, silent march around the perimeter of the square.

The rain has picked up in intensity. The sound of our footsteps in near unison on the wood is a counterpoint to the taut, random notes of raindrops exploding everywhere around us. The air is thick. The dank smell of the forest, rich and earthy. There's a mystical feeling to what we're doing here right now, as if it were a secret ritual.

Where did healthy ritual go, from my life? There were years when I went to synagogue, drawn to my mother's roots. I didn't believe Moses literally parted the Red Sea, but I knew those chants and prayers made me feel better, affording me a peace I had rarely inhabited elsewhere. A clearing of the mind. A feeling of the residue of the week having been washed away. Respite.

And yet, I never really felt I belonged there. It was as if there was an imperceptible whiff of Christmas tree instead of latke on my clothes in December. Some difference that raised suspicion on a subliminal level, something I always felt I had to apologize for, one more way in which I wasn't really good enough and didn't belong to anyone or anything.

What rituals did I turn to in later years, trying to recreate that same comfort? Running and biking obsessively, counting the minutes spent in exercise every day, the distance travelled. Fanatical preparation of the same meals, day in, day out. This much oatmeal. So many almonds. This much cereal. This lone, perfect oval of an egg. Weighing and recording and writing it all down, as if a biographer might want to read it one day.

You know the egg, that oatmeal: they were proxies, right? They were all Rosebud. They were love and guilt and more love, everything I could never separate from, all of it hopelessly scrambled.

231

Roy said it's not my fault. But *what's* not my fault?

The circle is moving more slowly now. Mick calls out for us to change pace. He reconfigures the group, and now half of us are walking in one direction and half in the other. We pass one another, neutral, unsmiling, two lanes of human traffic. The continual thudding of our feet against the boards. The pitch of the darkness, the tiny spears of rain. One expressionless face after another.

Mick stops us again. Now we turn to the person on the left and mirror whatever movements they're making. We're allowed to look at them directly. I end up across from a woman I don't know, shorter than I am, middle-aged, wearing a neon windbreaker. We put our palms up against each other, without touching, as if we're separated by a film of glass. I follow her lead, arms moving up, out, then around. Finding the confines of a space that eludes us, a space we can't even define.

There's been a film between me and everything for much of my life. It predates those awkward years in the synagogue, a girl with faint Ashkenazi features who spoke like a WASP. A girl who, like many girls, struggled to figure out exactly how much of her other people were entitled to. A girl who felt cleaved from the one thing she loved more than anything—her own family—because their lives were engulfed in flames, and she was the one who walked away when the metaphorical plane went down.

My partner makes circles in the air, like ripples in water. I try to emulate her every movement. She slows down, I slow down. Our breathing synchronizes. Spontaneously, our eyes meet. I wonder who she is. But besides wondering, I try to direct my attention to the fluid, dreamlike movements of our hands, as if she is painting me in soft brushstrokes, and I'm her self-portrait. Mirroring.

232

We have a whole mirror neuron network. It's a social phenomenon, something that allows us to thrive in groups where
empathy is adaptive to the survival of the whole. You cross your
leg, I cross my leg. You feel pain, I feel pain. What happens when
that network goes into overdrive? In cardiology, there is the
Frank–Starling law. When blood pressure is high, the powerful
left side of the heart is able to work harder, to bulk up. But after
years of this adaptation, pressure builds, then backs up into the
lungs, then overwhelms the right side of the heart, so the whole
system ultimately fails. What started as a single modification has
a series of irreversible consequences. Does that happen in the
brain, when we're pushed too hard, for too long, when we go for
years in chronically sleep-deprived states? When do those *early*
modifications begin to fail?

People here are dealing with everything from chronic
inferiority to severe anxiety to addiction to depression to crumbling marriages to the same depersonalization that first afflicted
me as a resident on the wards. Somewhere along the way, their
modifications have also failed. It must be the same for most of the
people I trained with and work with. But deep inside the labyrinth
of my own pain, I missed their grief too. Some of them could have
used my kind words, or an observation that they seemed sad, or
just off, or were drinking more than they had the previous year.
But I couldn't help them, because I was drowning too.

It used to hurt so much, that sense of betrayal. That no one gave
enough of a damn about me to try to poke beneath the superficial
first layer, the haphazard veneer. It's what grieved me the most,
that I could be walking around a hospital with a shattered heart,
and nobody could see. It only made me sure that my pain didn't
matter. Their blindness made me feel like even less of a person.

I think about my old friend from residency, Todd, the one who used to call me to chant on the answering machine that our lives sucked. Our lives *did* suck. But I think it was apparent that mine sucked more than his. Why didn't he ask if I was all right? I feel a sob rise up in my throat as I think to myself how abandoned I felt by him, how ridiculous I feel articulating it even now. I was a grown woman. He wasn't responsible for me. But Todd should have known. He had to know. Wasn't I even worth the discomfort of asking? We haven't talked for years. The last time he texted, it was my birthday. A lame text, a nothing text, a message I couldn't even be bothered to answer.

But then: *my birthday*. I think of a moment from the year Todd and I first met. We went to a craft sale, the kind you have to pay a lot of money to get into. We walked around the halls, lifting and touching pretty things. Every time I picked something up to admire, Todd would roll his eyes and say, "God, that's ugly," or, "Your taste is revolting." By the end of the show I was hurt by his barrage of criticism. I wanted to get away. I left him at the subway station and rode home fuming, vowing to cut him out of my life.

He called the next day. I was cool on the phone, pretended I had plans. Could he just drop something off for my birthday? A while later he came to the door, handed me a big bag brimming with little parcels. I pushed the layers of tissue paper aside.

I looked up at him, his face full of care and affection. I realized what he'd done. One by one, I pulled out all the things I'd admired at the craft sale. He *was* paying attention. In fact, he'd been keeping track of what I wanted, waiting for me to spell it out. So he could give it to me.

I forgot that he did that. I only remembered the hurt.

234

Mick calls out to stop mirroring. My partner and I turn away from each other. Mick asks us to stand, in complete stillness, to see if we can notice any feelings of connectedness that may have arisen during the mirroring. To just notice what's present for us, in this moment, right now. We're far enough apart in the darkness and the rain that I can't see other faces. They're soft, multicoloured blurs. I think of the faceless statue out by the pond.

It's raining heavily now. The two light posts on each side of the courtyard make wide triangles of yellow light. There's a military quality to our presence, as if we're a noble army. I read something before coming here about the "polyvagal" response of meditating in a group. The calm, parasympathetic effects of the body's mysterious vagus nerve when it's activated. I brushed it off as pap, but now I feel it unmistakably. It is, in a sense, a safety response. It might be adaptive. No animal wants to be separated from its pack. When it comes to survival, aloneness is the definition of vulnerability.

I realize it, as soon as the thought has formed. Somewhere along the way, I was separated from my pack. So were Roy and Jodie and Greg and Ikiru and Joss.

Now we're together, reunited. For one more day, here in the woods.

I don't know if it's enough.

o o o

MICK RELEASES US from marching. Like a flash mob, we disperse quickly. I go get ready for bed. The centre is eerily quiet. I change into my pyjamas and climb under the covers. I open the drawer in my night table and check my phone. There's a message from Eric that the boys are fine, a group text from my two friends back home. *How's the granola? Had your brain removed yet? We miss you at coffee.* I text them back: *Actually you guys it's turned out to be really good.* But I notice how even the act of getting my phone out of the drawer raises my heart rate just a little, precipitates a micro-blast of stress hormones. Who wants something from me now? Who's complaining about something? Who needs me to save them? Who's going to save me?

Is the problem that these messages are coming in, or is the problem my reaction? Every time someone lights a match, I come flying at them with a water bomber.

Is this a pattern for me?

I wish I could stay here more than a few days, in this suspended state, this cocoon of silence and stillness. And yet, I miss Eric. I miss my patients and my friends. Most of all, I miss my kids. I want to be with them, snuggling in one big bed, rain making orchestral sounds on the tin roof. I lie back on the pillow. A tear runs down the side of my face. I notice my chest tightening, a sensitivity in my teeth, a bogginess in my mouth.

Have I made my life harder than it has to be?

Maybe. But maybe I did it for a reason. Maybe I did it so there would be something to listen to other than wailing. Something to distract from the insurmountable losses, from all the grief I couldn't begin to articulate. A way to take control of the uncontrollable, like the band that played on the deck of the *Titanic* as it sank, drowning out the real emergency, the one it was too late to fix.

I thought it was my fault the boat was sinking. I believed all of it was somehow my fault. I believed my sister's cancer had visited us because of something I'd done. An assumption so obviously erroneous, it seems implausible that an intelligent child would hold it. And even though that fallacy felt as factual to me as my name or date of birth, because I didn't want anyone to think I wasn't an intelligent child, I never gave voice to it, never gave anyone the chance to correct or remove that ridiculous, mutated thought, and it worked its way into my DNA, into my whole life, and it just became a part of me.

And thus, I took on that same belief, subconsciously, for *every* person I cared for. Whatever ultimately happened to them was my fault. I was obliged to fix what could never possibly be fixed. Psychiatrists call this a repetition compulsion, a tendency to recreate a condition or scenario over and over, trying to resolve a leading note that lingers in your ear perennially, even when no one else can hear it.

I've been hearing those notes all my life. Just the way Wendy's radio and television played the same songs over and over, year after year. Just the way Wendy would call out sometimes from her bedroom, asking hopefully for the one hundredth time if doctors could fix the problem in her brain so she could walk again.

FOUR

24

Enough

The next morning, we shuffle into the Zendo in darkness. Above the high row of windows under which Mick and Ron are sitting, vestiges of pre-dawn light appear. Their faces are parked in neutral. I brought the wool blanket from my room and am using it like a shawl. I'm in a haze of silence and stillness.

I'm surprised by the juxtaposition inside me of peacefulness and undulating surges of emotion. I try to observe my thoughts, to identify what precedes each short spasm. Sometimes it's nothing I can identify, like a shadow on the grass of something flying over, high in the sky, gone by the time you look up.

Roy has a seat in the corner. He looks sad and tired. Ikiru is a few rows down, her black hair as big and messy as a crow's nest. I like seeing everyone in sweats, unbrushed hair, no makeup. We try to create illusions of flawlessness, to leave the impression that nothing bothers us or hurts us. We leave work, we go home, we fall to pieces. We didn't tend to our little green shoot. There's nothing in the garden. We don't know how to start again.

The surgeon with the brace limps in. His leg buckles a little with each step. When he's finally at the cushion, getting settled is a production. He sits down, folding one leg beneath him, and hoists the braced leg from the hip, bringing it up to the platform and leaving it out straight in front of him.

How has he put up with that for four days? The meditating, the walking. His leg must be swollen. Forget emotional discomfort, what's it like to sit here in deep physical pain? Hobbling back to the threadbare room only to toss and turn most of the night? How can his mind possibly do anything other than scream for Tylenol on schedule?

Mick is rambling about something now, using a bunch of Buddhist words like *dharma* and *mettha* that annoy the hell out of me, because I keep having to try to remember what *dharma* and *mettha* mean, which seems like an unfair extra step this early in the morning.

What happened to Wendy's brace? Did my parents throw it in the garbage?

How could they have just thrown it in the garbage?

What were they supposed to do with it?

Just that idea, that vision of my mom or my dad, setting that old piece of plastic in the trash, no leg left to cradle. And then the word *cradle* makes me think of her when she was a baby. Even then she probably still had that damn cancer growing in her head, just a little raisin, poised to cast a shadow for almost fifty years, for longer than that, really, because my children will always know that mommy had a sister who suffered, who had a bad thing in her brain and as a result liked country music and screamed and swore more than her fair share but loved the things she loved fiercely. All because of that first uncorrected mutated cell, one small thing gone horribly wrong. And mommy, as a result, always waiting for the next disaster, the dropping of the other shoe. Even when no one is wearing shoes.

Why am I here?

To learn to breathe, or to stop holding my breath?

I hear a sniffle a few cushions over. It's the woman who was my mirror last night. She's crying silently, trying to maintain her posture while she breathes and chokes back tears. I wonder if her mind is showing her a short film about medicine right now. I wonder what movie it is. I have Mike, Roy has Brian, Joss has the little girl who drowned. And then we have our personal collection of films: I have my sister, Ikiru has her mom. I don't know what films the others have. Different versions of the same script, though. It's in the early stages of dawning on me that if you could tap the phone lines of most of our private monologues, they would largely be full of indistinguishable chatter.

"We've been in silence since yesterday evening," Mick says. "You've had the chance to sit with whatever was present. Sometimes themes become apparent. Perhaps noticing now whether there are patterns that continue to make themselves known to you."

Mick, I know all about patterns, and not just because Roy got me thinking about it yesterday. I have what the shrinks call a drive for symmetry. I used to organize my dollhouses, my bookshelves, for hours, curating them to perfection. Dolls with expressionless resting bitch faces, positioned perfectly in front of food they were incapable of eating. Books arranged alphabetically and by size, sometimes by colour, less often by subject. It wasn't so much that I liked to have things organized. I liked to *look* at things when they were organized. I liked things around me to be perfect. It was a way to compensate for a chaotic environment. And now I work in a place where I can't compensate for chaos. Where there are holes in the plaster walls in patient rooms. Where people in stretchers are often parked out in front of the nursing desk the way you might leave an idling car. Where monitors beep, alarms sound, call bells ring, patients holler, and families line the hallways and sob. Where there is no order, only ongoing pandemonium.

Constant chaos on the outside. I can't do anything about it.

But what about the inside?

Mick takes a long, raspy inbreath, as if he's momentarily choking on his saliva. Good thing there are so many doctors here. We all sit in front of him, waiting. He clears his throat again.

Enough. These few words are enough.
If not these words, this breath.
If not this breath, this sitting here.

This opening to the life
we have refused
again and again
until now.

Until now.[*]

Now wait a minute. I haven't "refused" anything. I didn't choose this, the way I am.

---

* David Whyte, "Enough," in *Where Many Rivers Meet* (Washington: Many Rivers Press, 1990).

But I don't want to keep living like this.

That thought, like a gunshot. Not something you say with a sigh to a friend over a coffee break, or in a late-night semi-drunk text with your face glued to the white screen light. A realization, the sort of life truth that explodes like a Technicolor wasp's nest when you finally stumble upon it. Something you can never really put back in the box, once it's out in the daylight. Not a threat. Not idle words shouted in the throes of emotion, in a heated argument or a fit of exasperation. A real, fundamental truth. A basic, simple, noble truth.

A life I have refused.

Something huge is about to come to me, something bigger than this room and the viridian-Buddha-head hill that is just being illuminated in the dawn. Something uncomfortable I might not want to hear.

That I'm contributing to a lot of my suffering. That some is unavoidable, but some is a wall I've been running into at full speed. I crash, and go reeling, then run at it again, thinking I have to get through. As if that suffering could settle an account with the universe, the one where I received all those payments in error. Never considering that I could build a ladder to climb over that wall. That there are other ways to reach the other side.

o o o

BREAKFAST IS IN the dining room, in silence. Hard-boiled eggs, salt glistening on the thin membranes of skin covering the whites. The yolk, rimed with a dusky grey, breaking apart into lemony yellow pieces. Knives and forks against china make a pleasing, cafeteria sound. The sound of the herd grazing on its food, consuming in silence. I'm sitting with Greg and Jodie and the surgeon with the leg brace. I'm oddly comforted by their presence, even though we don't make eye contact. I like just knowing they're here. I think this is attachment.

A thin mist hovers over the field. Out the large plate-glass window, a deer trots across the pale grass. People look, and see each other looking, and soon everyone's heads are turned towards it. We watch it move effortlessly, sidestepping the stream and the road, then vanishing into the bushes.

I finish my coffee and get up to clean off my plate. When I push my chair back, it grates against the floor. Some people are still looking at the woods where the deer disappeared, hoping for an encore.

I go down the long hall towards the main entrance. That's when I see a mouse dart across the hardwood and into a guest room. Normally, I'd scream. A *C.S.I.*, 9-1-1 scream, but I don't, because we're in silence. Instead, I stand, frozen, probably with an idiotic emoji expression on my face. I always scream at mice. And yet, I just saw a mouse and didn't scream. There's an override in here somewhere!

We have a few minutes before we gather as a group in the great hall. I put on rubber boots and a jacket, and go out for a fast walk around the grounds.

On the pavement in front of the main entrance is something that looks like a hunk of tire. I go closer. It's a huge, horror-movie-grade black snake, lying in the sun on the warm pavement, a few inches away from a branch that must have come down in the wind.

A snake and a rod. Medicine's ultimate symbol: the staff of Asclepius, that consummate healer. Oh, universe, that's hilarious. And I don't scream at the snake either. If this were *Saturday Night Live*, in a few seconds I'd be face-to-face with a grizzly bear.

I come to the footbridge that leads to the little mill. The sun is hitting the water, a path of white light moving downstream. I hadn't really thought about the mill part of this place. All the land was donated by a businessman, Ralph B. Chapin. He lived here, with his family. I've seen a few signs, a commemorative plaque. Testimonials to his character: a good man. A Buddhist. A seeker.

I stand on the bridge. The mill is in perpetual motion, like a child's water toy. I watch it spin for a long time. I think about how the force of the water flowing is what turns the wheel. And the force of the wheel turning is what moves the axel, while another wheel hidden from view grinds and pulverizes grains, or stones, breaking them down from their original form, until they are ground very fine.

Shattered. No longer whole.

Serving another purpose.

25

You Are Still Carrying Her

S o what was that like?"

Ron and Mick are on chairs at the front of the room, a couple of new-age talk show hosts tossing a question to the live audience. They've brought us out of silence with a short meditation, and now we're debriefing. A lot of hands go up. Some people loved the silence. Some people were surprised by the content of their thoughts. Most agree it was tough not to use a phone, or to make eye contact. They worried about social graces. They wanted to compare notes.

The surgeon with the brace says, "When I saw the deer, I wanted you all to know about it. But then I shifted my attention to just noticing what it was like to see a deer."

I look over at Ikiru. She sees me looking at her and smiles. I smile back. Then I squint and touch my brow.

Did you take out your piercing?

She scowls at me. She touches her hair, as if drawing on it with a crayon, then shrugs with her palms open. I give her the finger. She gives me double fingers. Our faces split into wide, goofy grins.

The woman I was mirroring has her hand up, reaching for the microphone.

"I had kind of a profound moment with . . . sorry, I think it's Jill?"

I feel myself blush a little, a reflex since I was young. I give her a faint wave.

"We were mirroring each other in the rain. I just felt so close to her. And I don't even know her. I thought, how little it takes to feel close to people again." She's dabbing at her eyes the way she was in the Zendo.

I'm really touched. I raise my hand without thinking, and before I can change my mind, Mick is coming at me with the microphone.

"I realized two things." Everyone around me is listening intently. Even the quality of the listening is indescribable. Doctors normally interrupt patients after ten seconds. I doubt doctors wait ten seconds before interrupting each *other.*

"I realized there's a person who's constantly getting in my way. An important clue is she has blue hair."

Everyone laughs. Roy is looking at me like a proud father.

"But I realized something serious. I can't go on the way I have been. Doing call, those long stretches of barely sleeping. The things I tried to do for students. Not seeing my kids or being emotionally available for them. Some of the problem is me, and I totally accept that. But some of it is also medicine, and how we're teaching medicine. It isn't right that how we train has to maim many of us permanently. And it's coming to a head with all these other forces. I'm ready to start questioning *everything*. I need to tell the people who look me in the eye and say I'm not tough enough to practise or teach that the problem isn't *me*. I know it's not me. It isn't anybody in this room. Well, except for Jodie."

The room erupts into laughter. Jodie is scowling and shaking her fist at me like Statler on *The Muppets*.

Roy puts up his hand. The microphone is passed down.

"I have a confession. I broke the silence."

There are a few mock gasps.

"But I think it was the right thing, because we've been silent about so much for so long. Can I tell a short story, actually? Very short." He waits, and no one stops him. "It's the story of two monks standing at a river. Ron and Mick, you must have heard it before. A woman comes and asks if the monks would help her cross. One of them says no, because they aren't supposed to touch women. But the other one decides it's more important to help than to follow the rule. So he carries her across in his arms and deposits her on the bank on the other side. And the first monk is *pissed*. He won't talk to the second monk for days. They're eating supper almost a week later, and the first monk says, 'I'm still mad at you because you carried that woman.'" Roy turns to the group. "Does anyone know what the second monk says?"

He waits.

"He says, 'But you're still carrying her.'"

The room is silent. Roy is animated, passionate, no longer the sad old man I picture in a rented apartment.

"I've been thinking about one of my new friends here, and about all of us in the last twenty-four hours. *Why* are we still carrying all the people we've helped? This doesn't have to be the price of service."

251

Greg puts up his hand. "I like that story, because the person who is actually helpful doesn't get caught up in it. It's the monk who's obsessed with the rules who gets stuck."

"And we just might be a group of people who get obsessed with rules," Mick says, to widespread chuckles.

Greg nods so vigorously I'm afraid he's going to sprain his neck. "Both these monks live in my head. And they bicker until I want to just take a sedative to shut them up."

Ikiru raises her hand now. "I don't want to give them a sedative, because there might be merit in each of their views. I just don't want to get stuck on a passenger train with them."

Greg and Ikiru are both right. These guys live in my head too. I give them constant airtime. And all the thoughts they generate—I chase those thoughts like rabbits into holes. Judge something. Crave something. Do something. Get something. Change something. Then things will be *better*.

But better than *what*?

I think of all the patients whose lives I regularly implode with terrible news. If I died tomorrow, nothing would look as precious as today. Today would look like paradise.

Actually: it is vaguely like paradise. The slightly fucked-up, shattered-but-still-whole world of Jillian Horton. All of it. My family. My life back home. My new friends, who after only four days together are wearing their hearts on their sleeves. This place in the woods, with its smell like forest and coffee and patchouli and floor wax, and ponds and streams that amplify the rippling of the light. My own little room at Chapin Mill, with a bed and a warm blanket and a desk and lamp and window that looks out onto a hill.

Except I have to leave it, just as I'm clueing in to what it was.

But instead of descending into a pit of mourning, I notice the thought, and I wonder, *Why am I always pivoting from joy to grief? Why am I always making that my story?* Couldn't I possibly just exist in this one moment, for this moment, and be at peace?

Wasn't that what my old piano teacher asked me?

Could I have a good life?

o   o   o

I HAD THE most beautiful patient last year. In his twenties, trans, telling me I should refer to him as "he" for now, down from one of the northern reserves you can only drive to in the winter, when rivers and lakes freeze into ice road. His family decimated by addiction, violence, systemic oppression, intergenerational trauma. Using whatever he could get his hands on to dull the pain of his unspeakable excuse for a childhood. Heroin, liquor, Lysol, meth. A binge visiting cousins in the city. Admitted for a few days, vomiting up blood, his face puffy and miserable. Such a sweetness and tenderness about him, lying on the bed in his hospital gown, bemoaning its ugliness, rifling through his bed-side table so he could find a lipstick and show me what he looked like with his face on. Then telling me quietly, with downcast eyes, that he wanted to be a hairstylist; embarrassed, as if he had just confessed something totally unattainable, like he hoped to become an astronaut. His shy, peculiar request that I let him see me with my hair down.

Then, when I went to see him the next day, showing me a picture in one of his magazines, a cut he thought would be just right for me and the shape of my face.

What did I write on his copy of the discharge summary, adding

253

it at the last minute? A secret, heartfelt note, like one you might have passed to a friend when you were young:

Please look after yourself. It's ok to have a good life.

Bequeathing the words Don gave to me, even if I still couldn't believe them myself.

26

I Did Not Forget About You

Michael, would you be glad to know I still think about you? Your '70s glasses and your bad mullet? That I still have your postcards and the mix-tape you made me? That whenever I visit Toronto, I walk by the Chinatown store where we went one Saturday, you looking normal despite the gruesome sternal scar and the MedicAlert necklace, hunting for the weirdest collectibles ten dollars could buy? I'd like to tell you that in the Zendo, on these chilly mornings, your face comes to me. I'd like to be able to write that I see you, or I talk to you, or that we have a conversation, but that wouldn't be true. All I see are pieces of you. Your barking cough, the basins of mucus you produced before the transplant. That stupid shirt: *Nixon—he'll get the job done.*

If I could talk to you, I'd tell you I've always remembered what you said when it was finally clear you were on the mend and you'd survive the transplant, that you'd leave the hospital alive. We walked together to the end of the hall, to sit in two chairs on wheels by the huge glass window, to eat sawdust-like birthday cake off paper plates, cake I had really brought to celebrate the fact that you were alive. You rushed ahead of me to sit. I told you to slow down, because you were getting winded.

I know. I have to learn to breathe.

Would you believe I'm finally learning to breathe now too, Michael? It took me a really long time to get here, but I'm learning.

I loved watching you rise like Lazarus after you got those lungs. Hearing you make plans for a future that extended beyond the next twenty-four hours. You wanted to write too. You wanted to be a screenwriter. You had just started to scribble things down again, were just beginning to imagine a script about the story of your life. Before that, you'd been living in the space just in front of you, the way we sometimes think of writing: driving in the dark. You were afraid to drive in the daylight. You couldn't even let yourself look that far ahead, because it felt sickeningly naive to be hopeful.

Hope isn't naive. It's the only viable alternative. That's what I'd tell you if you were here with me at this faceless rock, looking out at this small, shallow lake pricked with rain. I'd tell you life doesn't owe us anything, but, as with my sister and brother, I still think it owed you more than you got. I'd tell you that you were one of my teachers. I'd tell you I'm sorry I failed you, I'm sorry to all the people I've failed, including myself, but I'm realizing that failure really is how we learn to do better the next time. I'd tell you I'm sorry I couldn't be there for you at the end, that you were my friend, that I did love you, that there is a kind of love between doctor and patient that is more personal, more timeless than most people could ever imagine. It isn't something we're supposed to run away from.

Something you wrote to me in an email: *When I was really sick the social worker sensed "guilt" on my part that I didn't feel I had the right to decide what happened in my own life 'cause what about the family?*

I wish I'd told you then what it's taken me all these years to understand: that it was *your* life. That it really did belong to you, even if it didn't always feel that way. That you lived it as well as any person could ever have lived it, under horrible circumstances. That if you're only living as a camera operator for someone else's story, you aren't really living. And if that's true for you, it must be true for me too.

You know what else you said to me in one of our emails? *You're so not like a doctor it's astounding. So where do you belong?*

I think I belong here, Michael.

And I did not forget about you.

Those are the words I've carried in my heart, like so many of us here.

FIVE

We Did Not Fail

The last day here is like the final day of camp, without parents. I can feel how everyone's thinking about the time right after lunch when the shuttle is scheduled to show up. People eat slowly but wistfully. We're worried about packing, whether flights are on time. We haven't left Chapin Mill, but we're mourning the place already.

My Affinity group meets for the last time. Joss and Greg and Jodie. There's a softness to each of us that wasn't there before. We settle in, noticing the breath. Noticing, for fleeting moments, how we're *noticing* the breath. Breathing, and breathing with one another, in and out.

"I don't care about reading the last poem," Jodie says. "I was wondering if we could just sit."

"Actually," Joss says, "can I read you guys something?"

Greg says, "Of course."

Joss takes a paper out of her pocket. She unfolds it slowly.

One winter's day
A crack appeared in all your lives
We tried to stop it from spreading
It was too late

I pumped her little chest
As cold as the ice she had broken through
But it wasn't any use.
There wouldn't be a spring.

Her sister tried to fish her out
But what a heavy burden for a child.
I hope that someone told her
What I had to learn myself:

You could not save her
And yet
You did not fail.

"Oh, Joss," Jodie murmurs.

"Don't say anything else, please. I'm not a poet or anything. I just really wanted to share it with the three of you."

Greg leans over, takes her hand. No one speaks.

Just being here in silence is enough.

Eighty-One

Ron asks us to form a circle with the chairs. Everybody sits. We take a moment to settle. There is one last exercise. It's called "Eighty-one." Many people are crying.

"Anybody can say a number between one and eighty-one. The only rule is the number you say has to be higher than the number the person before you said. And when someone says, 'Eighty-one,' the circle ends and we go home."

Some people look stricken. I can feel their separation anxiety hanging in the room.

Ron starts. "One."

There's silence for a moment. Everyone is processing.

Greg calls out, "Three."

Jodie: "Three-and-a-half." Everybody laughs.

Joss: "Three-and-three-quarters."

Roy: "Fifteen."

There's a little gasp. Roy shortened our last minutes together by an unnecessarily big interval! What an asshole! But his fifteen emboldens the psychiatrist from Northwestern, and he calls out, "Twenty-nine!"

It's fascinating to me, holding my own thoughts and noticing those of the others. I can see so clearly how they're drawing this all out, longer than it needs to be, how in doing so, they're not just adding to suffering but *creating* suffering.

All those years at the airport, saying goodbye to my parents. Waving goodbye, then coming back to the glass to see if they were still standing there on the other side, all those final hours and minutes. The grief lodged so tightly in my throat it threatened to cut off my airway. My parents at train or bus stations, dutifully waiting on platforms while I sucked back mucus and tears, my jaw rigid and aching from my perfect "Don't worry about me, I'll see you soon" smile. Waiting to see that I was all right, willing me to be all right, because they *needed* me to be all right, because, after all their loss, it was still an act of faith for them to send me out into the world.

All those minutes and hours when I dawdled at the school, waving at my boys, making the suffering of goodbye last too long.

It's not that the leaving doesn't have to hurt. But I see now that in the name of love we create a separate problem, a whole other universe of a problem.

Somebody calls out, "Forty-two."

"Forty-three."

"Fifty-six."

I can feel the deep tension in the room. There are people who are inclined to draw this out into tomorrow, to creep to the destination one number at a time. I can feel their near panic as we pick up speed. Their need for control. Or for the illusion of control. Or maybe just their need for an illusion.

"Eighty-one."

That was my voice. Firm, deliberate. It's over. Because I ended it.

There's a collective gasp, a hushed sigh. Ron and Mick stand up. Then everybody stands, and we hug and hold one another, laughing, weeping. A few people smack me on the shoulder.

Joss is pissed. "Why did you end it so soon?"

I put my arms on her shoulders. "I couldn't take it anymore." We lean in to hug, foreheads touching. "Then I realized I didn't *have* to take it anymore."

Ikiru has an early flight; she's getting an Uber with another doctor from California. It's outside, waiting. She blows me a slow kiss from across the room. I put a hand over my heart and blow a kiss back to her.

Jodie makes a beeline for me. "You're such a bitch!" She folds me into her arms.

"Don't I know it."

"Where have you been all my life?"

"I wasn't born for the first half."

"Did I mention that you're a fucking bitch?"

"I think you left out the adjective."

She gives me a kiss on the cheek. "If you need anything, and I mean *anything* . . ." Her words trail off. She tousles my curls, moves on to say goodbye to somebody else.

Greg is in front of me. His face is wet with tears, his voice hoarse.

"Thanks for doing that," he said. "I couldn't have ended it."

"I'm realizing we have to end it, Greg." I hold him so tightly I can feel the roughness of his beard in the crook of my neck. "Greg, *all* this shit has to end."

"Yeah." He sobs into my ear. "All this shit we do."

"That we didn't even know we were doing."

"And the stuff we knew we were doing. All of it."

"I know."

He takes in a few short staccato breaths, the way my little boys do when they're trying to speak through their tears.

"Because we were just trying to survive, Greg. Because it is a fucking *jungle* out there, and we did what we had to do."

"You bet we did." He steps back and puts his hands on my cheeks.

"We're saying everything we should have said out loud in the last twenty years."

"And we're going to keep saying it, okay?"

"Deal." I press one of my hands against his, hard, into my cheek.

"Christmas is coming, Jill."

"Any day now." I start laughing through my own tears. "I have to eighty-one you, Greg."

I kiss him on the forehead. He touches my blue hair.

I drift to the periphery of the hall, away from the group. I haven't finished packing my suitcase. I need a minute to organize the rest of my things. I make my last trek to the spartan room. It doesn't seem so small or empty anymore. I read the instructions on the back of the door that say how I'm supposed to leave everything. The wool blanket should be folded. Sheets should go out in a heap by the front entrance. The window should be closed.

I've been hoping for a knock on my door, and there it is. It floats open, and there's Roy, framed in the doorway like a familiar painting. We don't say anything. I run to him, and he comes to me, and we hold each other for a few minutes, or for all of time, until both of our faces are wet with tears, and I can feel his lithe body shuddering with emotion.

Finally, everything settles, and he whispers, "Eighty-one, Blue," and lets go of me, walks out the door and disappears into the hallway.

For a few minutes I stand looking at the empty door frame, but he doesn't come back.

Every time a patient is discharged, every time there is a death, housekeeping treks to the ward with their supplies and begins the ritual of wiping the room clean of all traces of the last occupant, preparing the room for the next one. How many patients have I cared for in the last twenty years? How many gurneys have I watched leave those rooms? How many people have I come to love and admire, their presence erased from the ward only hours after they left, or died, or were transferred somewhere better or worse? I'll never know the point of any of it. But maybe it isn't important that we know. I think of my beautiful sister and her short, difficult life. I think of my parents cleaning out her things after her death, her pictures and trinkets, her wheelchair and that stupid, futile brace.

Now in this room, I say to myself, *You don't wear the brace because you're going to walk again. You wear the brace because you are washing the bowl.*

Ritual is all we have. It's what keeps us from the abyss.

As I fold my blanket, check the drawers for things I might have left behind, then take one last look out the window at the little green hill, I realize something. *Eighty-one.* Eighty-one Falcon was my sister's address, the home where she last lived and died. What are the chances of that? It seems like one more mystical coincidence, one more thing that exists just beyond the margins of what we can apprehend with consciousness. The falcon, the ancient symbol of war.

Maybe I can say goodbye to that war now. Everything her life was and will never be, all the ways in which I failed and wasn't good enough, all the nieces and nephews I wish I had, the cakes and balloons, the ghost family I still imagine every year at Christmas. Going forward, just the way I am, carrying all my failures and losses, just the way they are. People I loved, and still love. Maybe I've set it all down here, just like I left my blanket in a square at the foot of the bed.

Acceptance isn't the same as endorsement. Leaving all that grief behind doesn't mean you loved anybody any less. But carrying it with you as you cross the river, drowning under its weight, won't bring anybody back. It won't.

I'm ready to go home.

My blanket is folded. The thin mattress is bare, and the pillow, ever so faintly stained blue after five days, is back at the head of the bed. I lift my suitcase. I turn out the lights. There is a tenderness in these preparations. I understand why the Buddhists pay close attention to such things. It's comforting when you know what to do.

What can happen in five days? It depends who you ask. But five days is enough to plant a seed. Five days gives you a place to start. It's not an ending. Instead it offers another possibility: a new beginning.

EPILOGUE

A Cure for Miracles

Most people experience major change in their lives as contemplative and incremental. This is how it was for me too. My first trip to Chapin Mill offered me a glimpse of how life could look if I found a way to reconfigure the parts of my psyche that were causing unnecessary pain. I came to the realization that reconfiguration was possible. But that realization had to dawn on me over and over again after leaving Chapin Mill. And I had to go back several times for the lesson to stick.

Change started with practice. A few minutes of breathwork, every day, usually on a cushion in my office at the lunch hour, observing my thoughts and feelings. Off the cushion, I chipped away at the questions Ron and Mick had asked that made me the most uncomfortable: Why would I refuse this life? What would be wrong with finding a way to feel better? At Chapin Mill, I had the insight that I wanted to live differently. I held on to that small epiphany. I noticed my thoughts, noticed my thought patterns, began to see which of those patterns led to impulses or behaviours that were counter to my quality of life. In the months that followed, I became less reactive—not always, but often. More and more, throughout the day, I noticed myself breathing deeply. In time, with less cumulative effort than one might think, I began to experience the subtly life-altering benefits of these simple, restorative practices. They were not a panacea. But it is also not an understatement to say that they have transformed my life, and, to some degree, my experience of being alive.

I also experienced a profound shift in my clinical life, a setting where I already felt emotionally capable and compassionate, a place where I didn't think I needed any help. Somehow, applying what Ron and Mick had taught me, I began to feel the suffering of my patients even more acutely . . . but also their strength and joy. I talked even less and listened even more. When I did speak, I took time to wait for the right words to appear, and I spoke them from the heart. I was more attuned to families, nurses, ward clerks. I cried more easily, and now, when grief came to visit, it didn't leave such a mess behind.

I took a year of teacher training with Mick and Ron. I logged countless hours working with groups of doctors, helping them learn new skills. I became a version of myself that felt more fully realized. I had done something I never previously believed I was capable of: I rewired my motherboard.

Then, in early 2020, just as I was putting the finishing touches on this book, COVID-19 changed all our lives forever. At my hospital, we braced for a deluge that we were initially fortunate enough to avoid. But in the late fall, our luck ran out. I had been off the inpatient wards, transitioning into a period of acquiring additional skills to support patients struggling with addiction. I waited to be called back in.

But the calls and emails that poured in had nothing to do with providing care to patients. My colleagues were desperate for anything that could help them cope with the crushing anxiety of working during COVID-19. They needed support. They needed a place for open dialogue. They wanted to learn mindfulness; they wanted to learn to meditate. And they wanted me to teach them how to do it.

So I did teach them. I *am* teaching them, helping as many of them as I can, supporting them in a way I could never have predicted, helping them manage their own stress and distress so they can take much better care of patients—and themselves.

A friend of mine noted that I seem much happier since I embraced mindfulness. He said he wished he could find his own miracle cure. I told him emphatically that mindfulness alone can never fix the systemic and organizational problems that have long been driving medicine's burnout crisis. But I think it can help us see things more clearly. And then, at least, we can stop waiting for transformation and rescue to come from the outside. In that sense, for me, mindfulness has been the cure *for* miracles.

o   o   o

PEOPLE OFTEN ASK me how my parents are since Wendy died. It feels strange to say they're doing fine, because the truth is more complex. But they are resilient people, and in the aftermath of her death, they've managed to constitute a life for themselves. They've both survived cancer, have travelled a little. My dad putters around the house; my mother bird watches. They are loving grandparents to our sons. They tend to Wendy's grave, and sometimes they run into one of Wendy's aides coming to leave flowers there too. They are so outwardly normal that it is easy to forget all they have been through. They have continued to wash the bowl. It has kept them from the abyss.

My brother, Chris, never recovered from his childhood illness. He was fully dependent on others for his care, distant, disengaged, long-suffering, until, six weeks into the COVID-19 pandemic, he died of unknown causes. A few weeks later, his ashes were placed next to Wendy's.

Heather is doing well. She has also had cancer. In light of our family history, she was beside herself at the diagnosis, inconsolable leading up to the surgery, predicting that cancer had spread inside her and that the end was near, even though there wasn't any evidence to suggest this was the case.

A few days before the operation was scheduled, she had a pre-op consultation with an anesthetist. The doctor told her what kind of anesthetic he planned to use. She said she didn't care.

Before he got up to leave, that anesthetist must have really *seen* her. My sister, scared, alone, her body slumped over, her face a mask of fear.

He said, "Heather?"

She looked up at him.

"You're a young woman, you're healthy, they caught this early, and you're going to be fine."

His face so kind, his words so authentic. The clouds parted.

Yes, she thought. He's right. Of *course* I am.

It was the work of Asclepius. A perfect blend of science and heart.

○ ○ ○

JUST BEFORE LIFE was imploded by COVID-19, I had my hardest case of all time. It had nothing to do with the virus. It involved a mother and her baby.

These are frightening times, when we are all struggling to keep the pieces of our lives from shattering into fragments, wondering what is left if they do shatter, and how we will ever return to the life we had before. We *won't* return to that life. We are never, ever going back. That is my most important lesson from Chapin Mill: the moment we accept this is when our next life begins.

The Very Last Story
Or, Turning Towards, Not Away

BY JILL H.

I

It was October. I was on call. That weekend there was a storm. I slept over in a hotel attached to the hospital, because the roads were clogged with snow as thick as plaster. I got my first call about her just before midnight, a woman in her thirties, a woman with cancer that had been diagnosed just before the birth of her first child. It was late, the resident was talking quickly, and I couldn't follow him at first. Sorry, how old's the baby? *Six weeks.* What happened six weeks ago? *She had a baby six weeks ago.* I kept thinking I'd misunderstood. So why isn't she going to Obstetrics? *She has brain metastases.* The resident repeating this patiently, at least three times. When did they find that out again? Thursday. *She learned she had brain mets Thursday.*

Today is Friday. She's in with vomiting, headaches, intractable nausea.

I ask the resident his plan. *Get it under control with medication, get her back home to be with baby.* Are there treatment options? *Nobody really knows.*

Trying to grasp this, as I hung up the phone. Forgetting her name and the details of her cancer, but remembering over and over, *her baby is six weeks old.*

I'm not prepared for how beautiful she is. I'm used to people looking sick. Yellow from liver damage, wasted from cancer or emphysema, bloated with fluid oozing out of their skin from heart failure. She looks perfect, as if there has been a mix-up, as if she is one of the nurses and the night had been so difficult she's just had to lie down. Lying still and silent because her head hurts so much. Headaches she's had for two weeks, intractable, intolerable; vomit spraying and hitting the wall, bits of food projecting across the room. Trying in between to hold her newborn baby for short bursts. She's had migraines before. Some people get them in pregnancy and postpartum, with all the hormone shifts. We call them *migraneurs*. But she isn't a *migraneur*.

She is dying.

We get her up to a bed on the ward. I call medical oncology, talk to the staff doctor for half an hour about our options. I call Radiation Oncology. They've already heard about her case. The staff physician has looked at the images. Her entire brain is full of metastatic deposits. *There's almost no brain left*, he says. But he doesn't say it like an asshole, like that doctor who said it about my sister. There's sorrow in his voice, the same bewilderment I feel. I look at the scans myself, sickened, photos of a crime scene. Black holes, tumours, like bubbles coming up from under water.

I'm still staring at the pictures on the computer at the nursing station when her mother comes and asks for me at the front desk. The mother has long, dark hair and a sweater covered in stars. She wants to talk to the staff doctor. I go up to the desk. Before I've even introduced myself, I am hugging her. We pull two chairs into a backroom by shelves full of hospital laundry. She puts her hand face-up on my lap, an invitation to hold it, the way my boys set their palms in front of me when they get a splinter, knowing Mom will fix it. I take her hand, and we sit on those chairs in the utility room, and I tell her I have talked to the oncologist. We're still going to try to get the swelling down, to get her to a point where we can give chemotherapy. She cries. I cry too. Her husband. Her mother. That little baby.

Is it a boy or girl?

It's a boy.

I ask his name, even though it hurts to know. I notice that it hurts. I don't want that baby to be real. If I don't know his name, he can stay an abstraction.

I learn his name.

We're still talking in the backroom when the nurse comes to find me in a panic, says the patient doesn't look right. I go straight to her room. Her eyelids are heavy now; she's not moving. I order Narcan, an opiate antidote, in case it's from the morphine. She wakes up a little, starts thrashing and hitting at the air, speaking nonsense. I know it's not the morphine. Her pupils are big and equal. I'm sure she's had a seizure. I call the ICU. Another scan. A central line in her neck, anti-seizure medications, pushing the only drug that could stop the swelling in her brain that's advancing like a wall of fire.

A baby at home. Six weeks old. He might be smiling now, a social smile. You still have to support his head.

Her husband, in the periphery of my vision. He doesn't know me. He has to trust me, is *forced* to trust me, a woman he's only just met. I want her to go to the ICU if she needs to, I tell them. Are we all on the same page? We are all on the same page. I *hate* this fucking page. She walked in here, for God's sake. She had a baby six weeks ago.

I am even more afraid of what's going to happen when we turn this page.

It all goes downhill overnight, faster than any of us expect, even with everyone on standby and ICU coming every hour and her moved in the interim to a bed where she can be watched like a hawk. The pressure in her brain so high. By the morning, intubated, ventilated, she's in a coma. Her family, around her bed, understanding on their faces, but not ready for the unfathomable, not yet; it's still too early. I go see them in the unit, and the mother collapses, sobbing into my arms. Tears pouring down my face too. The daughter still wearing a watch. A Fitbit. The futility of it. The cruel joke of that device. Her hair, brushed and pulled to the top of her head in a perfect, messy bun. The last time you get to do these things for someone you love more than anything, can you imagine? A fleeting thought: my mother doing this for Wendy for years and years. Brushing her hair. Washing the bowl.

I notice I am thinking about Wendy and my parents. That monumental loss.

It will pass. Don't run from it, let it be here. Tell it, *I see you.*

When I step out of the room, I'm blowing my nose. The young nurse doesn't look at my nametag, asks sympathetically if I'm a friend. I tell her I'm the doctor from the medicine ward. She looks surprised.

II

Two months later. A Sunday. Maureen takes me in, welcoming me at the door. We hug for a long time. David comes down with the baby, the house full of light and brick and hardwood. I'm so happy to see him. I give him a long hug too.

A huge canvas print of Hilary, from the service. Dancing, with that wild head of hair. Maureen gets another photo, shows it to me—Hilary in cute pyjamas, holding the baby just after he was born. Face upturned towards the camera. So proud. A mother for only six weeks.

Although you never stop being a mother. Or a sister. Or a daughter.

What happened that weekend? It's not the purpose of my visit, but we go over everything. Not with charts. We just need to talk about it, review it together, relive what happened at different moments that day. And the parts that happened before we met. The diagnosis. The timing of the delivery. The start date of the chemo postpartum, the staging, the other plans. What if? What if the baby had been induced earlier? What if they'd known earlier about those brain mets?

I tell them I know I did everything I could. We all did everything anyone could have done, and nothing could have changed the outcome. I know this unequivocally; I've been doing this for a long time now. I know they can see that I know it. Hilary is gone, but they're like my patients too, the ones I can still help. This is a part of closure, even though the wound will never really close.

Did I have any idea she was going to die the weekend we met?

No, I really didn't. I thought she had more time. I wanted her to have more time.

All the while, here and there, I'm noticing my breath. Noticing what's present for me. Calm. Grief. I can be present with grief. Grief isn't here to hurt me.

I turn towards it.

I watch the baby. Quinn. He's over three months old now. He tries to suck whatever gets within range of his pink mouth, those little ridges of gums just visible every time he cries out. I watch David give him the bottle. He holds him forward-facing and rocks him rhythmically. The baby is watching everything, his eyes latching onto each movement, his head turning in the direction of sound. David puts him in a bouncy chair under a mobile, and he flexes and extends his limbs, his whole body arching with excitement. Coloured stars and planets pass over him, drifting back and forth in the warm air from the furnace vent.

Maureen makes salad, and bread and cheese. She brings me coffee in a clear glass cup. There are chickadees at the window. It's hard to take my eyes off the baby.

Maureen asks if I remember the moment we met. Of course I remember. I tell her I could never forget her. I tell her I remember the stars.

The baby burps. He has no mother. David has no wife, Maureen has no daughter. The worst thing that could ever have happened has happened.

I have heard of doctors who quit medicine after a case like this. Grief brings the whole thing to a standstill. Seeing that little baby at night when you're trying to sleep, a baby you've never even met. The terror of the moment. The decisions made in a split second, decisions you train for years to make, situations with infinite variables. Did I do the right thing? Tears ambushing you in stairwells. Replaying that moment in the room when you realize she's dying, she's really going to die today, and it's my name on her hospital bracelet, and I don't want my name on any more bracelets on any more dead wrists or my signature on one more death certificate beneath the name of one more person whose story is going to shatter what's left of my heart.

None of that is present for me anymore. I'm breathing through it. I'm turning towards, not away. I did all the right things. I could not save her. I did not fail. This was never about me. Not in the way I thought it was.

Maureen says something to me at the door, something I don't really absorb until later that night, lying in bed, seeing *her* face, not the baby's.

As soon as I met you that day on the ward, I knew everything would be fine.

The paradox of those words. How did *I* make it fine? Nothing is fine. *Nothing* will ever be fine. She's gone, and there is that gaping hole blown in your life, and it will never be any other way.

But we're in a place where there is still bread, and coffee, and light coming in through a kitchen window—and a baby.

And there is still that other truth, the one Maureen has articulated. Stars in more than one dimension. Patterns we make in the darkness, things we do so we can find our way.

279

Author's Note

Confidentiality is a sacred tenet of medicine and also fundamental to the experience at Chapin Mill. Many colleagues and patient families generously consented to the sharing of their identities and stories without altering any details; their real names are used with permission (see acknowledgements).

Clinical cases where families are not named in the acknowledgements section are not based on specific patients, but they are representative of the many types of patients I have cared for in my twenty-year career.

Jodie Katz, Greg Collins, Mick Krasner and Ron Epstein all appear as themselves. Roy is a composite. Two individuals granted permission for their stories to be told so long as their identities were concealed; for this reason, Joss and Ikiru are composites, and the clinical cases they share are not based on specific patients.

Jonathan Starke allowed me to borrow his concept of a shared, real-time poem.

Aside from Nikki, who appears with her permission, any students or student interactions described in the sections about my academic work are necessarily composites drawn from my experience with the many and widely varied students I have taught and supported over the years.

Certain other names and details have been changed. Conversations and dialogue have been created in service to the story, but remain true to the spirit, individuals and moments of profound insight achieved at Chapin Mill.

I made more than one trip to Chapin Mill, and some events that occurred during subsequent trips are depicted as part of this first pilgrimage. The timing of my resignation as associate dean has been afforded some plasticity in relation to my Chapin Mill visits, as has the encounter with students discussing "Midlife with Dr. Horton," a scene that was inspired by two separate lectures. These minor adjustments allowed me to tell the story in a way that revealed the arc of insights and change, and enabled me to bring you, my reader, on this journey with me.

Acknowledgements

The list of people who made it possible for me to bring this book to fruition is almost as long as the book itself, but at the very top is my brilliant teacher, mentor, friend and coach, Stan Dragland. It is impossible to accurately depict the depth of his kindness, love and unshakable faith in me. He never stopped seeing me as a serious writer, and because of that, I could never find an excuse to stop writing. For the last twenty-five years he has offered me wisdom, insight, time, energy and six words that became a mantra: *Get it right, whatever it takes.* If I got it right, it's because of him, and I am indebted to him forever.

I am grateful to my cherished friend and teacher Mick Krasner, for being a co-conspirator and kindred spirit, and for changing my life with the first invitation to Chapin Mill.

My friend and mentor Ron Epstein was an enthusiastic and wise reader of a first draft of this book, and his belief in me as a writer gave me the resolve—and the courage—to get the job done. He is the one who helped me see that the story I needed to tell was right in front of me.

I owe a debt of gratitude to two brilliant writer friends, Leah Eichler and Nathinee Chen. In the years before I went to Chapin Mill, when I was fumbling with other stories of my life and dressing them up as fiction, they both took turns reading draft after draft of my work, critiquing from the head and the heart. Both are writers with tremendous talent of their own, and yet they devoted huge amounts of time to helping me get my own work off the ground. It is a favour I hope to repay one day.

I am so grateful for my literary angel, Jackie Kaiser. She conjured me up one morning on her way to the subway. That same day, this book showed up in her inbox, and then there was no turning back. She is brilliant, calm, laughs at my jokes and understood me from the moment she read the first few pages. There are few things more powerful than feeling we are truly known by someone else. Thank you, Jackie, from the bottom of my heart, for making all of this happen. Kismet.

Iris Tupholme, senior VP and executive publisher, gave me the best imaginable home, at HarperCollins Canada. She is the brilliant coach and book therapist every memoir deserves, and through her thoughtful questions and incisive comments, I came to understand even more about what happened at Chapin Mill. I am so grateful to have had the privilege of working with her and the benefit of her phenomenal talents and skill, not to mention her incredible kindness and warmth.

Julia McDowell gave meticulous, inspired notes that kept me chiselling away even on the days when I felt more like using a jackhammer. Allyson Latta and Noelle Zitzer guided me deftly through final edits and finishing touches. Everyone else at HarperCollins Canada supported this book and its message from day one. I will always be grateful for everything they have done to bring it into the world.

My dear friend, the writer and poet Molly Peacock, has been a lifelong inspiration. Her husband, Michael Groden, was one of my most important professors and cheerleaders, and he made me unafraid to take risks as a writer from early on. My other teachers at Western University helped me form the core belief that I was capable of being a writer, including Don Hair, Stephen Adams, John Lingard, Mary Neil and the late, great, infinitely compassionate Tom Tausky. My time at Western was also heavily influenced by the mentorship and support of two amazing trailblazers, the late Beryl and Richard M. Ivey, philanthropists who "levelled the playing field" between Oxford and McMaster, fundamentally altering the course of my life.

Many mentors in medicine have shaped my career in innumerable ways. It is important to emphasize that I benefitted from compassionate teachers, mentors, role models and program administrators at almost every turn in my medical education, at both McMaster University and the University of Toronto. The culture of medicine is universal, and the problems I have described with medical training almost certainly occur at every teaching hospital in North America. It is important to me to make the distinction between the people, who were often wonderful, and the system, which needs an overhaul.

Dr. Brian Goldman has given me friendship and encouragement at times when I needed it most and helped me figure out how to write in my own voice instead of someone else's. Dr. Sharon Straus is one of the wisest and most compassionate people I have ever known, and is still a friend, a guiding light and an inspiration to me after all these years. Dr. Howie Abrams was another larger-than-life influence on my approach to medicine, a kind of Hawkeye Pierce on a bicycle, who helped me find the conviction to stick it out when I was tempted to walk away. Dr. Brandon Meaney was my first great mentor, and I will always be grateful to him for showing me a way to be that was an extension of who I really am. Drs. Mike Froeschl, Heather Reich and Lynfa Stroud are just three of the many people who made residency bearable, with jokes that are still funny all these years later. I couldn't have survived it without you. I'm glad I didn't have to.

Don Henry, my first great teacher, has given me a lifetime of unconditional support and love, and opened my eyes to any number of intellectual and artistic worlds.

Maurice Mierau has worked with me to teach narrative medicine to doctors and has treated me like a serious writer from the very beginning of our friendship. Marina Rountree-James has been a sounding board for ideas and an incredibly intuitive beta-reader on perennially short notice.

I am also indebted to Heather Gibson, the incomparable executive producer of NAC Presents, and her team at the National Arts Centre, for bringing the *Insights: Arts, Medicine, Life* series to the stage. (Thanks for giving me the microphone, it's mine now.) Émilie Lacharité and Dr. Kirsten Patrick at the *Canadian Medical Association Journal* were the driving forces behind my work under the "Med Life with Dr. Horton" banner, including the "Dear Dr. Horton" column, a place where I eventually found my real voice. I'm so grateful to my friends and colleagues at the Canadian Medical Association and its subsidiary Joule for inviting me to join their crusade to improve physician health and the lives of all Canadians. I am proud to be part of their circle.

My friend and department head, Eberhard Renner, supported my taking an academic leave to finish this book, and more importantly, he has been a source of solidarity and shared values when it comes to the importance of the non-traditional work I am doing and the relationship between medicine and the arts. Several of my clinical colleagues and friends—Drs. Pam Orr, Len Minuk, Al (and Teresa) Bras, James Johnston, Martha Ainslie, Fred Aoki, Brian Schmidt, Don Houston, Sally Longstaffe, James Paul, Wendy Hooper, Debrah Wirtzfeld, Ken Van Ameyde, Joel Nkosi and Al Buchel—have been buddies in bad times, served as inspiration and created the circumstances for healing and laughter. Some have cared for me during tough times, and others have cared for members of my family with unbelievable skill and compassion, making all the difference.

My friends in allied health—all the helping professions—have enriched my life on every level. Many a difficult day has been made bearable by the kindness of my ward clerk friends, or laughter, debriefing and tears with my beloved nurse friends. Vanessa, Marcy, Egi, Eric, Diana, Blessing, Lisa, Lulu, Judy and too many others to name always managed to make the world brighter, no matter how hard the times. If one good thing has come from COVID-19, it is the sudden awakening in society to how much these people do for so many, and the grace and love with which they do it.

Many, many students have given my work as a teacher meaning and purpose, and I've learned from them too. I don't have to name them. They know who they are. Thank you.

My dear friend Grant Mitchell has passionately supported my artistic efforts on all fronts and given steadfast support and key advice during challenging personal times. John Myers, another friend and kindred spirit, has provided me with brilliant and deeply generous counsel.

Jim McLaren has been an irreplaceable champion and friend. Dawn MacDonald has been a key catalyst. My friend and producer Eitan Cornfield has been a source of inspiration and special friendship to me for twenty years. We're not done yet. Like so many doctors and health care providers, Alan Alda and his portrayal of Benjamin "Hawkeye" Pierce on *M*A*S*H* had a profound influence on the best parts of my clinical identity. I have benefitted from his immense kindness, as well as the important work being led by his team at the Alda Centre.

Many of my relationships from Chapin Mill have been sources of sustenance, strength and learning. Greg Collins and Jodie Katz will always be a part of my life; I am so grateful for their love, wisdom, laughter, friendship and openness to being themselves in this story. I am especially grateful to my teaching partner, Rick Szuster, for profound friendship and hijinks. Trish Luc was an important early mentor. I'm also indebted to Jonathan Starke, for his beautiful poem and the concept of working differently with things, and to so many others who have become part of my Chapin Mill family. The activities and teaching sessions described in this retreat are part of the Mindful Practice® program, created and developed by Drs. Ron Epstein and Mick Krasner while working at the University of Rochester. For more information about the Mindful Practice® program, please visit www.urmc.rochester.edu/family-medicine/mindful-practice.aspx.

ACKNOWLEDGEMENTS

I am filled with the deepest gratitude for my patients and their families. There are many, but in particular I want to acknowledge those whose surviving families have allowed me to share their true stories in these pages: Mike Yurkiw (Tom Yurkiw), Stan Bradley (Christine and Aidan Bradley), and Maureen and David, who will always have a special place in my heart.

So many other patients and families have changed my life by allowing me to care for them—too many to ever name. I will never forget you.

Thank you to The Arnold P. Gold Foundation and Dr. Richard Levin for honouring my work, championing me as a medical educator and leading the crusade for compassion in medical education and practice.

Thank you to my parents, who modelled unconditional love, unfathomable resilience, and even *M*A*S*H*-like humour in the worst of times, who did everything they could for all of us despite horrendous circumstances. If my compassion is exceptional, it is because of their example. It is impossible to do justice to the endless sacrifices they made for us, and how hard they worked to create the best opportunities they could for each of us to have a good life.

Thank you to my sister Heather, my friend and confidante, second mother to our children. I am so grateful for her.

Thank you to the many people who showed our family unforgettable compassion over the years—Wendy's devoted health-care aides, Iris Anderson, Dr. Michael Stambrook, Debbie Clevett, Dr. Liesel Moeller and Dr. Carine Minders. Also, Tommy Hunter and others.

To my loving husband, Eric, a devoted father to our sons, who has so often allowed my work to come ahead of his, including and especially my writing, and has made its success a priority: Thank you, dear.

And thanks to my three incredible boys, who have given my life purpose and healing, who have even done what they could to help me make time to write, who have made it possible for me to have a good life, because a good life means love.